my cool kitchen.

my cool kitchen.

a style guide to unique and inspirational kitchens

Jane Field-Lewis

photography by **Richard Maxted** and **Art Gray**

PAVILION

contents

introduction

This book looks at kitchens with style – not the sort of style you usually see in high-end magazines or manufacturers' catalogues but where their owners have created something unique and found their own self-expression, no matter whether the project is a thrifty option or an architecturally credible space.

We all have a kitchen, but in many homes they are a forgotten space where the cupboards alone have to tell the 'story', and personality and style are best left to other rooms in the house. In the following pages we're going on a journey to take a quiet and thoughtful look at some interesting people's kitchens and see what they have done. They are all people with something to say, and they've found a way of expressing their personality, individual style and tastes in their kitchens. They range from a high-end and totally awesome modern kitchen in a restored castle to a minimalist one in a cupboard; from an ultra-glamorous Californian beach front house to a kitchen in a former cinema as well as budget kitchens in owned and rented properties. My idea of style has no price boundaries, up or down, and no age barriers – style is not just the remit of the young upwardly mobile but something we all possess, whatever our location, age or income.

I hope you enjoy looking at these spaces and reading the tales that accompany them, and that you find some inspiration within them. Some of them have a cultural context, like the wonderful painterly kitchen of the Bloomsbury set at Charleston in Sussex, John Lennon's and Paul McCartney's kitchens from their formative years in Liverpool, or the one at Astley Castle, the former home of three English queens. Others express the interests and obsessions of their owners, from an antique dealer who lives with and eats off valuable Delftware to people who collect objects and can even create a kitchen inspired by the design of a saucepan. They each tell a unique story.

Over the years, the space we've allocated to the kitchen in our homes has changed enormously and reflects the transformation in our lives and times. It's interesting to take a look at our own world and how it has influenced how we decorate our houses. Some of us spend huge amounts of money on styling our kitchens, usually with fantastic results, but it's amazing what you can achieve on a much smaller budget and it's worth examining the spaces in which individuality and truth are valued more highly. The common ingredients in all the kitchens featured in this book, no matter how spacious, luxurious, simple or tiny, are the creativity and vision of their owners who want to make this space the living, breathing heart of their home.

All my preceding 'my cool...' books have also focused on individual style and how to achieve a stylish interesting life regardless of means. I started with caravans and campervans, moved on to sheds and now, finally, I've come indoors! I love photography almost as much as I love people themselves, and it's this wonderful mix of photography, individual style and people that really motivates and interests me, whatever I do. My eye is still on the aesthetic of whatever style I'm exploring, but I never preach about what you should aspire to, what is right or what constitutes good taste. Style comes in many guises, and a kitchen that captures your soul as well as suiting your budget is essentially what it's all about. This book reflects the personality of the creators of each of the featured kitchens, their objectives and needs and the intrinsic charm of their style. I hope it appeals to everyone who not only values the aesthetics and soul of their home but also looks to their environment as a source of inspiration and comfort.

I've been lucky to work with two talented photographers on this project, Art Gray in the United States and Richard Maxted in the UK and Europe. No matter how hard I try, there are always long road trips involved, which usually turn into their own adventures. This has been an incredible journey and I'm hugely indebted to both Art's and Richard's great talent, as well as the overseas photographers who kindly sent us their kitchen images and allowed us to include them in this book. And, above all, to the generosity of the kitchen owners who kindly opened their doors and invited us in to share their world.

This is far more than a conventional, prescriptive interiors book that focuses on just one style or approach. It is more human, individual and stylish. I want you to be motivated and inspired by what you see and read in the following pages, so that you can use this almost as a source book of ideas for developing your own personal style rather than submitting to the latest fads and fashions or losing your personal touch to a heavy designer dictum. I hope you enjoy the journey, too.

simple

Sometimes simple is best. We live in a high-tech, high-spec world surrounded by electronic gadgetry and wizardry, and many of today's kitchens are no exception. However, all the kitchens featured here share the natural beauty of simplicity and an honest authenticity. They are a celebration of getting back to basics and enjoying a more relaxing lifestyle with less fuss and clutter.

The two contrasting but complementary contemporary kitchens in an upmarket London townhouse both possess a simplicity of design and function. Clean, modern and no-nonsense, they are chic, well conceived and devoid of decorative flourishes. The aesthetic is in the detailed nuances and symmetry of the design. The vintage LA bungalow kitchen has avoided ripping out the original units and used them as a base for re-working this area into an artist's well-lit, studio-inspired space. The result is simple and doesn't overwhelm the space or the eye. Jenn Hannotte's Canadian kitchen uses well-used simple materials to create a modern homestead style, while Olaf Hajek's stylish and artistic Berlin kitchen utilises blackboard paint and plain white gloss units.

Sven and Gunilla's Scandinavian-style kitchen is a masterclass in simplicity, designed to blend seamlessly into the rustic environment. Out of a run-down wreck of a farm building, they created a timeless and harmonious space, which respects its agricultural heritage. Raw lime polished walls, aged wood and reclaimed materials are combined with old limestone blocks and farming implements to produce a natural and surprisingly modern-looking space. There are examples of hand-crafted super simple kitchens – in a rural Italian mill house that uses reclaimed wooden pallets as shelving, and Kaisa Luukkanen's made-to-order, removable kitchen that comes with just the pieces of equipment and storage you require. There is no hiding poor workmanship or a lack of finish – both kitchens are immaculate in their conception and creation.

Simplicity is seldom random and unselfconscious; on the contrary, it is often cleverly thought out, down to the last detail. Ironically, it's easier to achieve a multi-functional kitchen with lots going on in decorative ways than to pare everything down to the bare essentials. If you want a truly natural and simple look, you have to stand back and be objective – to know when to stop adding.

ann's los angeles kitchen

When Ann, an artist and designer, and her husband Clive bought this Los Angeles bungalow, it was pretty much in its original condition. This was a blessing, as they could renovate their new home, retaining its character and charm, while developing a more modern and lighter interpretation of the space. Built in 1928 to house McDonnell Douglas engineers who came to California to work in the burgeoning aerospace industry, the house is sited not far from the beach and benefits from cooling sea breezes and wonderful coastal light.

The original kitchen was fully enclosed, separated from the rest of the house by a solid wall and door. By removing the door and cutting away the left-hand side of the wall, Ann created a more open-plan space, improving the flow between the kitchen and the rest of the bungalow. And by opening up the roof space and removing the old flat ceiling – but leaving the roof joists that had supported it – it was taller and more airy. A central skylight was added at an angle, creating an asymmetric sculptural roof space, which, when dry lined and painted white, flooded the room with incredible light.

Now, many of us would have ripped out the old kitchen and replaced it with an off-the-peg melamine one, but not so here. The layout and design were functional and maximised the views, so in her clean and sympathetic restoration Ann retained most of the cupboards. The sink, stovetop and hood were replaced with modern stainless steel versions, and the counter tops were custom-made in white Corian to fit the space and have seen good duty for over twenty years.

style notes

Ann chose a neutral palette. Her eye for colour, tone and light is exceptional, and she wanted her kitchen to be like an artist's studio, a clean, light space in which she could create as well as cook, relax, play with the dog or pursue her love of flower arranging. It was a deliberate decision to make the space sculptural. The paint is a 'studio white' with no tint; the cupboards are pale grey with a slight gloss; and the white industrial flooring has a terrazzo feel. All the metal fittings (taps, doors and drawer knobs) are brushed silver in tone, minimal in design and high quality. This instantly adds glamour along with superior functionality.

By some well-thought-out but simple architectural changes, the room is luminous. The light pours in through the roof light and off the roof truss beams, and it's reflected off the deep return between the back door and windows. The floor reflects more light back upwards while the glazed back door opens outwards. The materials, too, are well considered. The half wall between the kitchen and the rest of the house has a piece of Carrara marble cut to fit neatly on top, adding texture, interest and more light. The principal materials are stainless steel, the white-toned paintwork and Corian work surfaces. And that's it – uncomplicated and restful on the eye. The narrow aluminium breakfast bar was custom-made and creates a balance in the room; the whole space is a useful area for working, eating and for Ann to display her artwork.

This kitchen is strongly architectural and relies on its form, light and space to carry its story. It has been on a confident journey from a traditional and unrestored space to this little piece of designer heaven. The somewhat counter-intuitive decision to keep the original units, rather than ripping them out, proved to be a very wise thing to do.

olaf hajek's chalkboard

A successful artist and illustrator, Olaf Hajek divides his time between his homes in London, New York and this stunning apartment in Berlin. His intricate and colourful art contains strong animal and plant life themes, mixing different places and cultures with myths and fairytales. His paintings are intriguing and you can't ignore them or look at them quickly – they draw you into a beautiful and complex parallel world.

It's always interesting to see how different artists' styles are represented in their homes and this is no exception. Although there are representations of the style of Olaf's work, this is a clean-lined, spacious and well-proportioned space in which his art has the starring role. As a piece of architecture, it is simple and refined and the overall feel is clean, crisp and fresh, but there are specific areas within this orderly space that encompass the details: the artworks, reference objects and books. They don't spill out all over the place but are neatly contained in painted wooden stacking units and bookshelves to create areas that feel more 'busy'. These collections are thoughtfully considered, not random or ramshackle; the bookcases house Olaf's unique collection of carefully arranged figures, cultural pieces and reference books. Although the individual items are important in themselves, the overall look and effect of the whole piece is equally fundamental.

Throughout the apartment there are warm-toned, natural wooden floors, with wide floorboards in the main rooms and herringbone parquet in the sitting room. Interestingly, Olaf doesn't use any colourful rugs to soften the space, as most people would; on the contrary, together with the furniture, the floor defines his distinctive clean and minimal style.

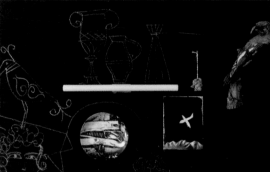

style notes

This apartment revolves around a long broad corridor leading to the dining room and, from there, into the adjoining kitchen. The wide open doorway between the two spaces fits with the general sense of flow and freedom of movement. With its large, chunky, sharp angles and neat glossy white island, the kitchen has a monumental feel. Its quintessential structure dominates and there are no details – no handles or decorative features. It is perfectly precise and contained without any curves; what you get here is just the neat angular form. However, Olaf has made a few concessions to comfort and relaxation: a low white bench extends along the length of the wall opposite the island, and there's also a classic Charles Eames armchair and footstool in the corner.

The chalk wall is a distinctive feature within the kitchen, fulfilling the purpose of linking the space with Olaf's art. This fun, unique and inexpensive feature of the wall space touches on some of Berlin's history and its fascination with graffiti and instinctive art. It's a safe zone for experimental scribbles and trying things out – they may be great art or just impulsive squiggles. As Paul Klee memorably said: 'A drawing is simply a line going for a walk'.

There's a remarkable feeling here of freedom of expression and that things can be changed and erased – real art isn't precious or permanent but a living and ever evolving creative process, which is adventurous, experimental and fun. As well as being functional, there's the space and the opportunity just to be and to think in this kitchen, to doodle on the chalk wall or to draw properly – you always have a choice.

london townhouse kitchens

The owners of these two contrasting but stylish kitchens run a monthly dining club from their home in central London, and they engaged Project Orange, an architecture and interior design studio, to design not only a small extension providing more living space but also to reconfigure the house to better accommodate guests. The architects accomplished this by shifting the main kitchen to the first floor alongside the dining room and reintroducing partitions on the ground floor to create an office and TV room. An infill extension was added at the rear with a huge roof light to form a new day room, and another smaller kitchen was located in the basement to serve the ground and lower ground floor spaces.

The upstairs contemporary steel kitchen was designed with standard products while introducing detail nuances for a bespoke and more quirky aesthetic. The owners worked within a predetermined budget and all the base units are Ikea, while the dining room units have bespoke Douglas Fir tops and are cantilevered from the wall. The work top is specially made in integrated stainless steel. The underfloor heating installation required the removal of the existing floorboards, which were re-used in the new furnishings and a bespoke door lining to the dining room. The owners use this every day as well as for their monthly supper club.

Both kitchens are built from simple elemental materials, each with its own distinctive texture, the cool luminous light reflecting stainless steel, reclaimed wood with its strong grain and knots on show, and simple plain white units. These form the bones and structure of the rooms. All the colour comes in the doors – in the basement kitchen they are green. And against this elegant palette the owners' collections of books and artefacts are cleverly grouped to create areas of stronger colour and add a sense of the individual to the space.

style notes

In the upstairs kitchen, there's a symmetry between the lines and balance of the work surfaces, racking and shelving, and with the materials in the cooking and dining areas, making a visual connection between the two rooms as they share the same space. The doorway between them is deliberately wide because the owners didn't want a 'show kitchen' – their guests need to see and smell what is going on. As they're both involved in the supper club, they need to be able to entertain and converse as well as cooking the food – the wide doorway makes this easier.

The dining area has a very unstuffy feel. It's clean and modern, with 14 stacking old school chairs, purchased in a local market. When they're not all in use, they can be stacked away in the corner. The floor is made from a uniformly grey linoleum, but in the kitchen it has more 'grain', making the surface non-slip. The same white industrial-style light fittings are used throughout. Repetition and the use of multiples play an important role in creating an architectural language, accentuating rhythm and consistency.

Although the kitchen is all steel and quite industrial looking, its aesthetics, such as the central hanging pan rack and steel trolley, prevent it looking too austere. All the 'tools of the trade' are on view, so you can just grab a pan. Every utensil has a dedicated home and there's no grovelling in over-packed drawers and cupboards looking for a spatula. This is a no-nonsense kitchen: there are no fussy decorations, the walls are painted a simple flat

white and, instead of a complicated window treatment, there's a chic plain translucent roller blind. The size of the window relates well to the door opening. Your eye is drawn towards the light source – the window and the perspective created by the two long work surfaces and the similar lines of the wall shelves only enhance this effect.

In the downstairs kitchen, the original floorboards were removed to install an underfloor heating system. Instead of dumping them in a skip, they were recycled to make the worktop, splashback and shelves. Even the plinth under the units was made from a floorboard to keep the composition balanced. The chunky work surface and shelf are 75mm (3in) thick. This was a deliberate ploy, not only for aesthetic reasons but also to stabilise the edge of the floorboards – creating a thick sandwich achieved both outcomes. The deep window has an important function in this basement kitchen. Although it opens into a small courtyard without any views, it floods the space with light and gives it a luminous quality. The materials in the lower kitchen have an appealing simplicity and honesty about them – the floor is polished concrete, creating a robust yet reflective surface.

This kitchen works successfully following its transformation from a tiny scullery into a wonderful top-lit space. Every detail, no matter how small, has been thought through carefully and by getting those quiet details right, the proportions and balance working together and the amount of daylight flooding in, both kitchens are comfortable and desirable spaces.

jenn hannotte's pioneer style

Toronto-based interior designer Jenn Hannotte wanted a kitchen that wouldn't be permanent. Styles come and go, and not all of us want to invest in a kitchen to last a lifetime. Jenn didn't have the budget for a 'full meal deal' renovation and opted for a temporary solution, keeping the existing layout but adding inexpensive materials and units. By cleverly using plywood and inexpensive mass-produced units, she created a surprisingly elegant space. Because it wasn't designed to last forever, she could experiment with ideas and materials. She decided on pale birch plywood from the local hardware store for the walls to create warmth. Other budget-watching measures included fixing the plywood 10cm (4in) from the original wall for pipes and cabling to run behind it, and base units from Ikea. Jenn's design philosophy is admirable: a willingness to work within a small budget while pushing the boundaries creatively. This non-conformist approach proves the humble can be elevated and the everyday made beautiful.

style notes

This might be an affordable kitchen but it's still a highly individual and homely space, based on a collection of simple elements, such as the uncluttered white china on the wooden shelf. No attempt is made to hide the simple brackets or to add hi-tech elements. Style-wise, Jenn wanted to bring a tongue-in-cheek elegance to the rusticity of the space. There is nothing pretentious here – the bare light fitting is almost sculptural. This space forces you to look at the details more than the big picture. It's good to keep things simple and just love the things you have, paring them down to the ones that have significance and special meaning. It takes discipline, but it can be wonderfully zen and cleansing to live small and lean with less 'stuff'.

This hand-made kitchen was designed by the Helsinki-based interior architect Kaisa Luukkanen, who likes to create intellectual objects that contribute ecologically to the essentials of our lives, adding comfort and functionality along with a lightness of touch. In the early stages of a new project she usually has a clear goal in mind, and during the design process she tries to find the right materials and work methods to achieve it. The plan for this kitchen, in an office within the Old Customs Warehouse building in Helsinki, evolved in this way. Hand-crafted out of wood, it is completely modular, focusing on lighter materials and functional storage.

It's an example of her versatile Cargo Kitchen, which is totally modular and moveable. The three core pieces – work table, steel-topped appliance unit and storage unit – can be customised to individual requirements. They are all designed to be moveable between different homes and are sufficiently flexible to accommodate changes, updating, additions and reconfigurations. This style is particularly suited to open-plan spaces, where the kitchen will always be visible, as well as small studio apartments where space is at a premium.

Kaisa has created a brand that emphasises the high quality of the manufacturing process but is distinctive from the conventional aesthetics of furniture design. Essentially, this custom-made kitchen offers you a well designed, simple but relatively blank canvas on which to add your own finishing touches. The design credibility and sense of style are implicit, and it doesn't take all the oxygen out of the room. It respects and leaves space for your own expression, too.

hand-made
helsinki kitchen

style notes

The experience of using objects and their visual aesthetic are equally valuable to Kaisa. This kitchen is made of solid birch, a wood that is plentiful in her native Finland and which ages beautifully. Its strength and good matching qualities lend themselves to her style of kitchen construction. Whatever wood she chooses – birch, oak, black alder or ash – she prefers a natural finish, such as oil or wax. The flexible long table unit, which comes in three sizes, can double up as a workspace. The design and finish are light and delicate – visually, they have a clean aesthetic and don't impose on the space.

This kitchen is cavernous with the architectural characteristics of an old factory or industrial building. It's an honest space with exposed iron girders – the structure of the building is there to be seen. Two black metal industrial-looking pendant lights reference the style of the building and hang low over the table. Together with the mismatched materials, styles and ages of the stools, bench and chairs, they create an arty, creative and collegiate space. It isn't formal or imposed but has more of an inclusive, relaxed feel.

Along with the stainless steel work surface and lamps, the free-standing steel trolley, which is used for open storage, sits well with the birch wood, the other key material in this space. Overall, the colour scheme is neutral – it doesn't shout. Colour and tone are added by means of the light shades and the clean-lined kitchen pans, coffee pot and kettle on the wall shelves. All have a rounded sculptural form and are practical rather than overly decorative objects.

rustic swedish farmhouse kitchen

Sven and Gunilla's home is a 300-year-old farmhouse, timber-framed and mud-bricked. It was a wreck when they bought it, but during the extensive restoration, they were careful to retain the cultural values and heritage of this cluster of buildings and to use traditional methods and reclaimed materials. Their greatest challenge was how to find the right balance between what to save and restore, and what to replace. When planning their beautifully conceived kitchen in the old barn, they wanted to stay as close as possible to the original features and opted for a simple, durable design that would blend seamlessly into the rustic atmosphere.

style notes

This kitchen is timeless and natural. The materials, textures and colours were all purposely chosen by Gunilla and Sven. They wanted a flexible, functional and atmospheric space and opted for raw lime polished walls and aged wood to create an authentic feel. They even gave a new lease of life to some farming implements, such as an old metal heating lamp used for keeping piglets warm. They just changed the bulb and hung it low over the sink. Many of the unusual objects were collected on their travels. The porcelain sink was purchased in China; an old Danish ceramic pot nestles beside a Thai basket and an Austrian wooden plate. On the table sits an intricate Thai food cover, while the glasses in the metal holder were picked up in India. The carpet is an old Kelim and there's an appealing Spanish wine jar in the window. All these disparate objects have been skillfully woven together to create an elegant space. There are traditional Scandinavian elements, such as the red Falu linseed oil paint on the trestle legs and the table glasswear. There is an innate generosity in this space; it's a welcoming area.

Katrin Ahrens is an artist who works in wood, fabric and ceramics. Whichever materials she fashions, she has a passion for simplicity and a talent for creating beautiful functional pieces out of reclaimed materials. This kitchen is in her old mill house in Italy. She was viewing another property when she spotted this abandoned house in the distance on the other side of the valley and knew instinctively that this was the right place for her. Katrin relishes a challenge and she quickly began work on restoring it. However, she did not attempt to change the original configuration, and the kitchen opens up onto a long exterior balcony. Her ethos is to create limited edition pieces that are unique and site-specific, taking their cue from the proportions of the room. She has stayed true to her design compass and philosophy in her own kitchen, creating a very understated, natural look.

katrin ahrens' mill house

style notes

To be truthful to the origins of all the materials in her kitchen, Katrin used them as her guide when selecting the colour palette. All the tones have a gentle quality and are very pale, neutral or wood. The walls are pleasingly uneven with a distinctive surface that 'looks like ricotta cheese' and, rather than using a brilliant white modern finish, Katrin has painted them a more gentle greyish tone of white. The pieces of wooden furniture are nearly all of her own creation, using reclaimed and recycled materials. She has long collected interesting pieces of no longer wanted old wood from carpentry workshops and abandoned buildings. The kitchen doors, for example, were originally shutters in an old farmhouse. Katrin looks at each piece and instinctively knows what she needs to do with it. She doesn't like to over-complicate and over-construct an object – simplicity is key for her.

Interior designer Emma Wilson bravely left her London city life behind to embrace a simpler lifestyle in a Moroccan coastal village. She has a passion for stylish interiors and vibrant colours, which she has used to great effect in the holiday homes she rents out. When she bought this house it was an open-plan lofty space in characteristic 'Beldi' style, but she had a clear vision of how she wanted it to look and set about ripping everything out bar the four external walls. For the walls, flooring, kitchen island and shelving, she used 'tadelakt', a traditional Moroccan lime plaster, polished to a smooth finish. In the local style, there's a central courtyard, which acts like an extension to the kitchen. It reinforces the sense of space, volume and light and provides an additional dining area. This kitchen has a comfortable, homely feel, which is rich in texture, from the glossy smoothness of the floor, walls and work surfaces, to the wooden ceiling with its joists more like natural tree trunks. It's a place to chill and take time out.

style notes
The textural rugs enhance the sense of comfort in what could otherwise be a room of hard surfaces. This happy conflict of soft and hard, smooth and textural, cold and warm is reflected in the furnishings. Shiny translucent acrylic stools are placed at the kitchen island, and on the shelves are hand-thrown local earthenware tagines. Emma's love of vintage and texture is seen in her squashy sofa, while the table and chairs follow the 'hard' angular theme. The large dining table is a key piece and balances the island. Like the rest of the space, the kitchen isn't over-filled. The shelves are uncluttered and there are few appliances. This is a contemporary stylish place, which makes sense of where it is and feels like a comfortable home.

hand-crafted moroccan kitchen

eclectic

Some kitchens defy current tastes and derive their uniquely individual style from a variety of different elements and a diverse range of themes and sources. You need the courage of your convictions and a strongly ingrained sense of personal style to think outside the usual box and create a truly eclectic kitchen, but that is what the owners of the spaces featured in the following pages have done. Some have been designed or evolved organically around their collections of objects or artworks; Robert and Lucie Gordon's love of art, antiques, crafts and colour brought their north London kitchen together. This hybrid space melds Robert's Scandi minimalism with Lucie's exuberant sense of colour. It's a work in progress – an ever-changing space where they try out new ideas.

Other kitchens have been inspired by a strong graphic feeling for design. The visually intriguing Antwerp kitchen with its distinctive checkerboard finish is a delicate balancing act between understated minimalism and sophistication, the repeat pattern creating a sense of modest elegance. Likewise, the townhouse of style guru Abigail Ahern is a testament to her design ideas and principles. Her basement kitchen is a visually rich and comfortable space with an original mix of objects, each of which has a story to tell.

What makes all these kitchens so interesting is how they remain functional working spaces while embodying an aesthetic manifesto for living. Several of them have evolved over time rather than being an 'out of the box' approach. The kitchen at Charleston contains decorative furniture, ceramic tiles and crockery created by three different generations of the same family. The Boulevard Leopold Antwerp kitchen was designed back in the 1920s and, despite a renovation, has retained the original kitchen-dresser style units for storing china.

These are unique spaces and not to everyone's taste, but I admire their boldness and collated nature. The colours are vibrant and the materials more resourceful, while quirky items are added and removed, so the rooms rarely stay exactly the same. We look at a range of kitchens, from a hand-built house in Hawaii with natural earth walls, to the artist David Bromley's former Australian kitchen with hand-painted striped walls and artwork covering almost every inch.

antiques and crafts london home

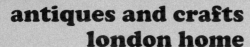

A love of antiques, craft and colour has brought this kitchen together. In a north London house, antique dealer Robert Gordon and his wife Lucie have created this colourful and intriguing space whose look has evolved gradually. Different styles have come and gone, ranging from Robert's love of pale-toned schemes to today's exuberantly coloured versions fashioned by Lucie. Where some folk might want to harmonise the colours and tones, no attempt has been made at matching or co-ordination, and it's none the worse for it.

Lucie's training in textile design and work over the years with antique and vintage textiles and costumes have contributed to her passion for rich colours and textures. Her eye is honed and her ever-developing taste is part of her life. She isn't faint of heart when it comes to choosing courageous colours, nor does she call in the decorators; she just clears a small area and starts to paint. To complete the whole job in one go is overwhelming, so she works her way around a room step by step. It's all about creating atmosphere as well as something appealing to the eye.

The kitchen was designed to be a 'working' space with everything on show, from the laundry drying rack to the antique crockery. Rather disarmingly, valuable antiques, furniture, ceramics and paintings are intermixed with everyday utensils and other items. All are in daily use, to be sat on, looked at and enjoyed. The family even nonchalantly eats pasta off nineteenth-century Delftware. 'But I wish Robert had told me how much it was worth before I put a bowl in the dishwasher and cracked it. We still use it most days, cracks and all,' Lucie says cheerfully.

style notes

Robert and Lucie replaced the old cupboards with one linear run of white, simple high-gloss units, and hung three vintage 1960s orange ceiling lights in a row above them. However, the kitchen units are not the main players here. In fact, your eye has so many places to go that you hardly notice them. The horizontal clapboard walls, clad in tongue-and-groove panelling, proclaim Robert's roots in Scandinavia. He wanted to create a Swedish cabin look, not in a perfect way but something more homely and ramshackle. The walls were originally painted a lighter tone, but when the end wall got the orange treatment it was so powerful that the clapboard was toned down by painting it a muted sludgy green.

The Swedish influence is evident throughout. The precious seventeenth- and eighteenth-century Delftware pieces are mixed with modern pottery and ceramics found in local antique markets. The table and chairs reflect the unusual mix of high and low art. Two of the chairs are Ercol originals and the white circular table is an Aaro Sarrinnen piece. There are two vintage school desks, with yellow formica surfaces on which the couple's children draw, paint, or have fun with beads and crafts. Next to them is a traditional Swedish pull-out day bed. The 1950s metal cupboard stores a collection of well-used crockery and glassware. On top are four decorative stars made from old potato crisp packets, one of Lucie's fortieth birthday presents.

Rather than a job finished, this is an ever evolving and changing space. The couple are constantly trying out new ideas, adding furniture and replacing paintings and ceramics, and, of course, the option of painting a wall a different colour is never far away.

Charleston was the country home of the Bloomsbury Set, a progressive group of artists, writers, intellectuals and philosophers who rejected many conservative values of Edwardian society and embraced a more Bohemian unconventional lifestyle. From 1916, Vanessa and Clive Bell lived there, together with Duncan Grant and his lover David Garnett. Virginia Woolf, Vanessa's sister, lived nearby, and the house became the nucleus of a loose group of friends and relatives – an inspirational place where they could develop their aesthetic and intellectual ideas. The Bloomsbury Group believed that art was a much broader medium than painting and sculpture, and at Charleston the walls, doors, furniture, textiles and ceramics became their decorative canvases and a domestic object was as important as a classic piece of art.

Charleston was a working studio as well as a home, playing open house to friends, relatives and colleagues who wished to contribute to its artistic content. In spite of its simple exterior, every inch inside, from the painted furniture and doors to the frescoed walls, reflects the movement's, painterly, decorative style. And the large, square kitchen is no exception. There are two small windows through which the farm cows once stuck their heads, and the size of the room, the Aga and large square table create a comfortable warm space. The large dresser, painted in the 'house style' by Vanessa, decoratively sets the tone. Hand-painted tiles behind the Belfast sink are by Quentin Bell as are the rows of mugs hanging on the staircase.

charleston bloomsbury style

After Vanessa and Duncan's deaths, the house fell into disrepair, but the Charleston Trust campaigned to restore it to its former glory. Pierre Matisse donated one of his father's sketches and thus history repeated itself and the house came full circle, back to post-impressionism and the modernist movement that had fascinated the Bloomsbury Group artists.

style notes

It's not often that a kitchen can resist fashion long enough to allow three generations of the same family to have a hand in its decoration, but that's what happened here. It is as much an intrinsic part of the 'Bloomsbury' style as the other areas of the house. Like much of the artwork in the house, the natural structure of the dresser has been made into a feature with the panelling emulating a picture frame. Within the inner painted frame are still lifes of flowers and luxuriant English fruit bowls. The painting was executed by Vanessa on canvas before being set within the panelled recesses. Her son Quentin painted the splashback behind the butler sink and the tiles lining the cooker chimney breast. Hanging on the rough sawn planking of the staircase are rows of his ceramic mugs. To the left of the sink, the linen curtain was created by Quentin's daughter Cressida, a widely acclaimed designer. The stylised leaf outline and curved teardrop design on a natural background is characteristic of the Bloomsbury style.

The room is a comfortable space – large and square – and the rustic wooden table follows suit. The kitchen is painted a chalky matt white whereas the doors are a cool, flat grey. Apart from the ceramic tiling, all the textures are matt, helping create a warm atmosphere. Vanessa's maxim that 'Wherever your eyes should fall, they should fall on objects of beauty' is brought to life here. Even the quirky ceramic light fittings, inspired by upturned colanders, are reproductions of the house style, casting a transformational sparkling drop effect. Like the rest of the house, this kitchen, with its imaginative decoration, extends the concept of credible art far beyond framed canvases and conventional artworks into a domestic living environment.

david & yuge bromley's painterly kitchen

Just a quick glance tells you this kitchen was developed by a creative mind. The home of artist David Bromley and his fashion designer wife Yuge is a unique space. Initially, this was their weekend retreat, but they now live and work here full-time. They love paint, and decorating and renovation are tasks they happily embrace in preference to full-on building work. They prefer to 'build' the space by using furniture, artworks and unique bits and pieces, finding the right place for them in the house and then creating the space around them in an architectural way.

style notes

This is a deeply textural and layered space. The walls are painted freehand with white stripes upon a black base, creating a loose, painterly wallpaper on which everything else sits. Artworks are positioned on top or the stripes are painted around the art. This painterly style is a way of democratising art, reinforcing the notion that creative endeavours are as equally valid as paintings, sculpture, textiles, furniture or crockery. This is art totally in its own context, filling the space rather than just displayed as areas of interest on the walls. It identifies the room as a space in its own right rather than a purely functional area for food preparation. Similarly, the use of rugs adds a poignant sense of a lived-in room rather than a clinical space.

The floor has been left in its natural wood finish like some of the work surfaces and blinds, softening the strength of the black and white stripes. David has an eye for antiques and artworks and enjoys collecting ephemera, mixing disparate pieces from different eras and styles. Such juxtapositions are hard to invent, but in this quirky, art-filled house, there is an integrity to the collection. David has applied his own sense of the aesthetic to this visually rich environment to create a space he loves. It's one of the most amazing kitchens I've ever seen.

Abigail Ahern, style maven, interior designer and entrepreneur, is someone who practises what she preaches. In her Victorian terraced townhouse in east London, she has made a stunning kitchen/dining/living space, which is a testament to her design ideas and principles. The house is decorated throughout in her signature style – dark walls in cleverly varying tones; rich and highly textured stone, worn leather, sheepskin and velvet; and deeply tactile fabrics and rugs, punctuated by bright, vibrantly coloured artworks and objects. However, this isn't a place without humour. Abigail likes rooms to have their own personality and she plays with their scale, adding layers of depth and wit. It isn't all about colour and texture – the furniture is positioned cleverly to create a deliberate meandering path; it slows you down, forcing you to observe specific pieces rather than walking past without noticing them. This pattern of moving resembles that of a gently flowing river, but it isn't distracting – it's a visual treat.

Abigail works here, teaching design classes and using it as a living example of her philosophy for creating a comfortable home. Her upstairs office is on a mezzanine level, created by adding a vast two-storey, glass-walled extension. This is one of the magic ingredients in this amazingly successful space. Cleverly lit by daylight and small decorative lamps, the dark colours of the walls are transformed into a canvas against which the furniture and objects sing out.

Abigail's kitchen wasn't conceived as a self-contained separate space – it fills the entire basement area of the house. However, unlike many basements, it's not dark and below ground level because the front garden slopes down and connects to it via a huge glass wall, thereby cleverly blending the inside of the house with the outside world. The kitchen is at the front of this open-plan space with a dining area in the middle and a lounging area at the back.

abigail ahern's london townhouse

style notes

Unlike so many people who opt for a slick, polished, expensive open-plan kitchen, Abigail has created one that is alive, dense and visually rich with the comfortable feel and atmosphere of a space in which you want to spend all day pottering about. Whether making coffee, flicking through recipe books for ideas for supper, chatting with friends, playing with the dogs or just lounging, this flexible and multi-functional space works on all levels.

However, the kitchen hasn't always looked like this. When Abigail purchased the house, it was 'a sterile white space...as boring as hell'. The original island and units were 'bog standard' basic Ikea products, but instead of using the doors that were supplied, she had plain taller ones cut from mdf. She added deep stainless steel work surfaces while retaining the polished concrete floor. The kitchen was functional, but for Abigail it lacked character and visual interest, so she painted the mdf doors in her signature dark colours, and created areas in which to sit and think or dream, or to have conversations. She added small console tables with interesting lamps and artefacts around the walls, and glass domes, unusual cooking pots, vintage lamps and piles of cookbooks, flowers, plants and candles to further enrich the space.

OK, I hear you say, but everything's out on show even though there's a lot of proper cupboard space. However, there's method in Abigail's madness and all the objects on display have been carefully selected and positioned. She has honed her eye throughout the various stages of

her career, working as a picture researcher, stylist, interior designer and shop owner. The images on her blog and website as well as her shop displays have to be updated regularly, as new products are introduced and the seasons change. Likewise, the items in her kitchen are placed equally carefully and strategically in a decorative way, and little visual stories are created out of books, candles in textural glass votives, spices in tiny handmade dishes, and bowls of tangerines...do you get the idea?

The concrete floor is no longer bare, and several small rugs of different designs, colours and textures have been specifically placed to relate to the spaces between the units and the furniture in the rest of the room. Abigail says: 'I think that the kitchen is often the most neglected room in the house...people just don't know how to decorate them'. Well, they could certainly learn from her example and take a leaf out of her book.

This is a delightful and inspiring space. It has courage and originality. The kitchen units are not destined to be major players in this scene – they merge effortlessly into the background structure. Layers of stories and narrative are added on top, but these can and do change regularly. Abigail believes that you shouldn't be able to 'read' a space instantly, and she has designed her kitchen in such a way that 'your eye is pulled in different directions'. This isn't any old kitchen that you pop into just to make a coffee or grab a snack. It's an important and integral design statement of Abigail's aesthetic manifesto for living.

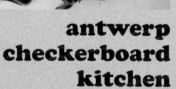

antwerp checkerboard kitchen

This historic 1890s Antwerp merchant's house is now a B&B of the most desirable kind. It is an elegant building, with large well-proportioned rooms and high ceilings and its history resonates in the original stonework, wrought iron, marble, grand fireplaces, cornices and woodwork. Martin, its owner, transformed Boulevard Leopold into three apartments. On the ground floor is a huge sitting room, painted a dark but relaxing sludgy green. Stylish and visually intriguing, it is dark and dramatic, with sharp glints of light striking glass, and metallic silver and gold. Velvety red Amaryllis, richly coloured wood, worn leather and frankincense candles are the finishing touches to creating an atmosphere that engages all our senses.

Dotted around the large comfortable sofas and vintage '50s chairs are collections of objects that convey a sense of history – old photographs, crucifixes from a monastery that was closing down, a giant stack of logs and piles of antiquarian books. They are grouped in multiples rather than spread out in a linear fashion, and there is a fascinating blend of the beautiful, the macabre and the religious.

The kitchen has a lighter and fresher tone. Built as part of an extension to the back of the building in the 1920s, it is decorated in its entirety in ceramic-glazed white and blue tiles. The original glazed dresser-style cupboards were moved into the anteroom. Statuesque pieces, with detailed woodwork, they are extremely grand. Between the sitting room and kitchen is a large dining area. Old Belgian café tables have been repaired with red marmoleum surfaces, and there are charming old restaurant banquettes and simple wooden chairs.

style notes

The original 1920s glazed ceramic tiles spectacularly cover every surface – the floor, walls, ceiling and even a small cornice and picture rail. Off-white with a delicate blue geometric repeat pattern, they follow and pick out the structure of the room, weaving their way around the corners, chimney breast and door openings. The floor tiles have more of a honed finish and their pattern, instead of the conventional repeat checkerboard, is slightly looser with each blue tile spaced between three white ones. The rows containing blue tiles are interspaced with entirely white rows, and the pattern is repeated with the blue tile set diagonally within the surrounding white. Three edges of the floor are bordered by a dense decorative feature, consisting of a solid line of blue tiles with an inner checkerboard pattern, which picks out and defines the wall line. The tiles are the big players here, setting the tone of this elegant room.

The new base units do not visually overwhelm or overly fill the space. These modest, unadorned cupboards, topped with Belgian blue stone, create a simple yet strong line along the length of the kitchen. Above them is a painted shelf, and sitting on and hanging from it are vintage silver tea and coffee pots. These are not the highly polished perfect ones that you might see in a stately home – they are tarnished, slightly dented and life-worn. It's a wonderfully light space, with part-glazed, beautifully panelled doors at both ends. One set leads into the back garden, while the other provides easy access from the hallway. A period deeply-rounded topped cast-iron radiator provides a contrasting finishing touch, running the length of the window, and fitting below the original wall panelling. This is a truly stylish kitchen – refined and sophisticated yet surprisingly understated and kind of minimalist. A real visual feast.

David Easton and his wife Cindy are experts in 'rammed earth', an ancient building method using a compacted mixture of natural materials – typically, natural mineral soil, gravel, clay and sand. They conceived this unconventional project of a rammed earth surf/beach house on Maui, the second largest of the Hawaiian islands, using the shipwrecked Robinson Crusoe's shelter as their inspiration. From their home in California, David meticulously planned this project, packing four shipping containers with tools, plumbing and electrical materials, a solar water heater, pre-cut pieces for cabinets and doors, furniture, appliances, crockery, bedding and towels – everything needed to construct and fill a spacious house, apart from the local volcanic earth for the walls, floor and plaster, which would be excavated from the site. After fulfilling their transportation purposes, the containers would serve as a temporary shelter before being used to build a one-bedroom cottage.

The first structure to be built was the central kitchen/dining/living pavilion, and they started with the galvanised corrugated steel roof, with its large overhang, supported by steel poles. Now sheltered from the rain, the wall construction could begin. The soil garnered from levelling the ground was mixed with gravel and sand to create the mix. It took six weeks to complete the first pavilion. It had doors, windows, sliding patio doors that, in effect, open up the walls, a cooker, a refrigerator and a bathroom. Using the pre-cut pieces, assembling the kitchen was relatively quick. The interior 'earth plaster' had a base layer of long-chopped straw and a mix of soils, sand, Hawaiian cement and hydrated lime. For the top layer, a traditional Japanese plaster was used – pure earth with less straw and no cement or lime added. The walls were left in their natural finish, as were the roof interior and flooring.

hana beach rammed earth surf house

style notes

This is a touchy feely space with interesting, varied and multi-faceted tones and textures. The floor shines, the bamboo and roofing sheeting add a vertical ridged texture, and the lime and clay plastered walls have a warm, chalky matt softness. This kitchen is in context not only with its location but also with its structure and manufacture. It isn't creating another message; it's all about where it is and what it's made of. David and Cindy planned it as a ship's galley. The frames for the cupboards were constructed from recycled lumber back in California and then finished in Maui with locally sourced bamboo screening or open shelving. The concrete worktops were formed and poured on site. Nearly all of the appliances, plates, glasses, and cutlery were shipped over in the containers, as were the Viking range, the fridge, dishwasher and range hood.

The locally purchased comfortable futon sofa, rattan chairs, side tables and tall bar stools are all fashioned out of bent bamboo with timeless traditional bark cloth upholstery. Reproductions of the kind of furniture that David grew up with in southern Californian beach houses, they have a relaxed style that says, 'The ocean is nearby'. The large patio doors slide open to an outdoor area, which is decked out with a table and chairs plus a simple woven lounger chair where you

can lie back, sip a coconut-based cocktail, watch the colourful birds and listen to the waves crashing on the rocks below. In the winter, David and Cindy use the binoculars, in easy reach beside the lounger, for whale watching – grey, blue and humpback whales migrate all the way from Alaska to calve in the warmer waters around Maui. This outdoor area, protected from the rain and trade winds by the large overhang of the roof, is the perfect location for the washing line of surfing and beachwear fluttering in the breeze. They especially love the sound of rain pattering on a tin roof – rainfall on this part of the island is monumental; gentle showers pass quickly with a soothing sound like the sea while heavy rain is short-lived but dramatic and noisy.

This truly inspirational hybrid of self-build and eco house has been created with enormous sensitivity and care – for the best and most altruistic of reasons. What David and Cindy were trying to prove was that small shipping containers could be packed and converted into affordable disaster relief housing – and they were right. They are determined innovators who never stop searching for new building solutions, no matter how elusive. Whether it's a case of being shipwrecked on a tropical island or broken down in a desert, they believe that they can always find a way to create a shelter from the resources within their watershed, and this wonderful house is a testament to their resourcefulness.

tiny

Tiny does not necessarily mean inferior, less stylish or functional – often, less is more. The initial reaction of visitors to the tiny space-age style Hivehaus kitchen is usually 'Wow!'. However, successful small space design requires some forethought and detailed planning to make it work for you – on every level. And the owners of the kitchens in this section have come up with some ingenious design solutions for making maximum use of the available space. Although small by most modern standards, all the kitchens are engaging and aesthetically pleasing in their own way. Some are infinitely flexible, opening up into larger living spaces like the modernist Chert kitchen. At the other extreme, the minute Hivehaus kitchen is the size of a modest wardrobe and almost disappears into the wall when it's closed. The trick is to create a comfortable space that doesn't feel cluttered, and the key to success is usually simplicity and following your own sense of style, whether it's vintage and quirky like Rosie Wolfenden's colourful Le Creuset inspired kitchen or impossibly elegant and decorative as is the case with Virginie Manivert's tiny Parisian space.

Colour is an interesting element. Few of us can be as daring as Virginie, who seized her paintbrush and...voilà!...created a sublimely stylish blue kitchen. The result is unbelievably calming and soothing on the eye as well as aesthetically appealing. Conversely, the artist Mathieu Mercier's kitchen is a white minimalist dream, but far from being a blank space it's full of light and exquisite detail. These kitchens are less accommodating to the evolutionary approach of a look that develops gradually over time. They need to be clever spaces, both in terms of their practicality and aesthetics. The smallest and simplest of spaces need considerable deliberation as to how to make good use of what you've got without forgetting your own style in the effort to squeeze everything in. I guess that is the actual point: to be sensible about storage but still add character, not forgetting room for you, too.

What all the kitchens featured in this section of the book prove is that by trusting your instincts and not slavishly following fashion, you can transform even a tiny space into a warm and cosy yet stylish and elegant environment, which retains its functionality and where you can enjoy cooking and eating.

stylist's parisian blue kitchen

When Virginie Manivet moved into her third-floor classic 'Haussmann' Parisian home, it was painted white throughout. The two apartments on her floor had once been a single larger one, and when it was subdivided the bathrooms and kitchen took most of the impact, while the spacious, elegant salon with its comfortable proportions and original fireplace remained. In scale and feel, it is stately, resembling a well-loved miniature château albeit in more human proportions. Initially it was the salon that received Virginie's 'blue' treatment, but that didn't work. Nevertheless, the 'blue phase' continued. When Virginie feels inspired by a particular colour, she has to start painting immediately, even if it's the middle of the night. The tone of blue she fell in love with came from a swatch, and she asked her local paint shop to match it. And this was the germ of the idea for her tiny distinctive blue kitchen.

Versatile and artistic, she trained as an interior architect and has also worked as a stylist and personal shopper, sourcing beautiful interior artefacts. It takes considerable energy and vision to be always researching, but for Virginie it's the gateway to an exciting world where she can live in the moment. Sometimes there's a key creative inspiration that sparks and guides your tastes and artistic direction. The French novelist, poet, designer, artist and filmmaker Jean Cocteau has always been a major influence on Virginie's style. The materials, colours, tones and richness of Morocco and Spain also have a stylistic 'pull' for her and have all found resonance in the decoration of this apartment. Spanish terracotta casserole pots, earthenware cream and terracotta marbelised plates, and the original terracotta-and-white checkerboard floor set the tone. The metal garden table is painted in the same colour. And, of course, there's that blue! It's such a rich colour with a lot of red in it – a tonal counterpoint to the terracotta but with the same visual weight, making it equally powerful.

style notes

The tiny kitchen runs off the entrance hallway, and it really is very small. It was created out of part of the bathroom of the former larger flat, and you can still see the original tiling and recessed ceramic soap dish on the far wall, all painted blue. Although the blue and the terracotta are the main players here, note the use of black, which has been added as punctuation, in a similar way to a defining line in a Cocteau painting. For Virginie, it acts as a contrast: 'If you paint something black, like the chair in the kitchen, you lose the detail and see only the form – the curves of the back of the seat are like a backbone...I like to find the human form in things.'

Virginie may be super-stylish, but she also has a sense of humour and she doesn't like life to be too serious. She looks for threads and, for her, one inspired idea leads to another and weaves its way through her life. The terracotta bust of Saint Tropez, which stands neatly in the box shelf, is her little homage to many happy childhood summers spent in the town that bears his name. 'I have a strong relationship with the sea and the scents of the south.' Similarly, the little statue that lies in what was once the old soap dish makes her smile. Made by a friend out of terracotta mixed with mica

crystals (because 'all my life I have found stones with mica in them'), it fits the dish perfectly. The mosaic vase on the lower shelf was also brought back from the south of France.

Virginie eats at the small oblong metal folding table in the kitchen. It's unusual insofar as it's the type and style that you would more usually see on a small outdoor terrace; its corners and edges are gently rounded, and the tin folding legs add a sense of lightless to the piece. In keeping with the limited palette in this kitchen, it has been painted terracotta.

The classic French centre-opening window looks out over the internal courtyard, and as Virginie's apartment is located high up on the third floor of the building the quality of the daylight is very good. The unlined curtains add a softness to the kitchen – they are vintage toile de Jouy, and were found in a local market. The fabric is cotton, the print terracotta.

This is an individual kitchen, which speaks of a strong personal design ethic and approach; the decoration has courage and it tells a story. Virginie has a truly creative disposition and, like the rest of her home, this tiny space is a unique expression of herself, her art and her work. The basic ingredients are not expensive units or an upmarket and fashionable re-fit but a collection of functional, meaningful and aesthetically pleasing objects, which, as a whole piece, form this unique, charming and super-stylish place.

The quality most of us seek to represent in our kitchens is a functional space with an aesthetic sense that reflects our style and works on a practical level. Sometimes this is tinged with aspiration; at other times, it's the practicality that overwhelms. In the case of artist and sculptor Mathieu Mercier and his wife Moraima, their kitchen takes on an even more complex and personal representation.

Their home is a 'Haussmann' Parisian apartment overlooking a park. Built in the nineteenth century to accommodate the rising bourgeoisie, these apartments are characteristically formal and although they are still elegant and stately, they were designed for a different time. For their early occupants, food preparation and cooking were not a social activity and kitchens were kept deliberately tiny. For this artistic and cultured family, the aesthetics of a more open and light space were a major consideration. They wanted their kitchen to have purity, clarity and balance as well as being functional and pragmatic. Mathieu has incredible spatial awareness and an acute sensibility about space and its possibilities. So the original super-tiny kitchen and the equally tiny adjoining office space were opened up and its transformation began.

Mathieu values and appreciates other artists' work. His impressive collection has evolved and grown by exchanging his own work with that of others. He doesn't live with any of his own artworks, only those he has acquired from other artists. It's against this background that his amazing white kitchen emerged. A deceptively simple and visually clean space, it's not only a counterpoint to the incredible art in the rest of the apartment but it's also open to the light and wonderful views.

mathieu mercier's minimal kitchen

style notes

When Mathieu and Moraima planned this kitchen, they envisaged a clinical, minimalist space with no appliances on show excepting the oven. In fact, Moraima describes it as a 'cheap and fancy kitchen'. Working within their limited budget with some architects who were paid only in artworks, savings were made by using Ikea roller units and cabinets from Darty, one of the leading European household appliance groups, while no expense was spared on the exquisite white Corian work surface and sink. And rather than having the usual chunky squared-off edge, Mathieu designed the shape of the worktop edge himself, using the edge of the dining table as his template and inspiration. From the surface there's an initial small soft bevel and then a tapered receding edge. It's beautiful on the eye, and the light falls over the different angles with a softness, making the surface look thinner and adding a delicate beauty.

Natural light was an important consideration in the planning of this kitchen as well as making the available space feel open and spacious rather than enclosed. A long landscape area and proportioned internal window were added between the kitchen and the hallway, which is also open to the main living rooms. This serves to boost the light in the kitchen as well as affording it a view of the distant park, while linking it to the rest of the apartment. Viewed from the hallway, the window is surrounded by a colourful wall of art books, thereby creating a library within which the kitchen scene resembles a big screen showing a real, living drama.

The presence of art is never far away. On the window ledge is a Didier Marcel tree trunk sculpture – a gesture linking the exterior park landscape and kitchen interior. Mathieu already owned the Donald Judd drawing; it found its own place in the kitchen when it was completed and is a perfect fit. Moraima describes it as 'almost like a kitchen thing, a drawer perhaps', and although it's a minimal piece of work in this environment it becomes almost interactive and integral to the space around it. All the 'objects' in the kitchen are artworks in themselves, and each one sits quietly and comfortably within the space. This is not a contrived placement – the individual pieces work naturally together, as though joined by an invisible thread. The print is a Donald Judd, the lamp is by Verner Panton, the fruit bowl was designed by Jasper Morrisson, the glasses were made by Joe Colombo, and the stools are Konstantin Grcic creations.

Roll up the roller cupboards and voilà! Behind them are all the everyday kitchen items, electrical appliances and utensils that are usually out on show: the coffee maker, kettle, crockery and foodstuffs, all ready to hand as and when you need them. However, when the doors are rolled shut, art, light and exquisite line and space are the masters here. This innovative kitchen exhibits an exciting network of art, architecture and design, embracing what works for the space with no pretension or illusion – the everyday is combined with the unique. It is a truly aesthetic space which is used, loved, accessible and approachable.

hivehaus kitchen in a cupboard

The almost universal initial reaction to the tiny kitchen in Barry Jackson's Hivehaus is 'Wow!' The concept is based on a hexagonal pod, similar to the honeycombs built by bees. It's affordable, moveable and flexible. More pods can be added and the design re-configured accordingly. Based on an equilateral triangle, each pod is, in effect, six triangles fitted together. Barry, who is naturally creative and practical, set about building this prototype. Inspired by the modernist principles of Bauhaus, it has its own simplicity and functionality without ornamentation.

It's a simple yet flexible concept: the wall panels are each made of three identically sized sections. The owner can choose the materials for each section – fully or partially glazed, or a simple solid wall – and this configuration can be altered later on, depending on budget or necessity. The internal walls are mdf, insulated with a steel clad exterior, while the roof is fibreglass with domed, circular central skylights, which flood the space with light.

Barry wanted the kitchen to fit flush along just one wall rather than a conventional layout of units extending into the room. He called on the expertise of his friends Mick and Emma Culshaw, who had designed a similar tiny kitchen but along more traditional lines. Barry had a specific style in mind, drawing on the 1970s Gerry Anderson TV show 'UFO' and the Matti Suuronen flying saucer-shaped prefabricated house designs of the '60s and '70s with a touch of 'Blake 7' thrown in for inspiration. Taking these reference points and reinterpreting them, they set about designing a simple space-age form, which Barry christened 'future retro'.

The kitchen is highly engineered, beautifully constructed, balanced and finished; when closed, it almost disappears into the wall. It has a strong visual presence, helped by the lack of handles and the matt paint finish and colour. And although it's tiny, it's not squashed or lacking in equipment; on the contrary, it's an area of great style, simplicity and beauty.

style notes

It is rare for a kitchen to be thought of as an absolute whole – as one unit rather than an assembly of its component parts. Being seen as an integral part of the Hivehaus meant the materials, colour, textures and form all needed careful consideration. Measuring 180cm wide x 210cm high x 650cm (70 x 82 x 256in) deep, it's about the size of a modest wardrobe.

A vintage mid-century studio couch by Ercol, which was already owned by the family, provided the inspiration for the details of the design. It now resides in the main sitting area. Its curvy wooden arms and simple tapering legs were key to developing the rounded shape of the exterior corners of the kitchen as well as the double curves of the interior shelving design. The modern but retro-styled fabric covering the upholstery of the couch also informed the starting point for the paint colour choices. Barry wanted a neutral exterior when the kitchen was closed, so that it almost disappeared into the wall, but with more impact when opened up. To achieve this effect, he chose a richer, more vibrant cerulean blue for the interior back wall.

With a gentle touch, the bi-fold doors, with built-in neat shelving sections, easily swing open, either to totally extend or half open and fold back on themselves to form wall cupboards. The decision to leave the shelving in its natural oak finish was made by Mick, the craftsman who helped design and build the kitchen. This helps make the shape of the shelving, with its distinctive double curved corners, a visible and contributing factor to the design. Rather than being low-key, barely noticeable shelves, they are there to be seen and play their part in the whole aesthetic. Using a gloss finish and no obvious handles is a classic piece of small kitchen

advice, but it hasn't been followed here. Barry felt that look was too contemporary; he was after something more elusive and retro. Consequently, he used a warm grey with a subtle sheen, an eggshell finish formulated for spraying on to the doors to softly blend with the walls and tonally sit with the oak flooring. Gloss is the traditional means of reflecting light around a space, but this treatment has a very soft lustre and a more recessive finish.

Even the kitchen table has been designed in line with the design principles and stylisation of the main kitchen unit. Hexagonal in shape, it has ovoid 'Futuro' shaped details along each edge, which form an open shelf beneath. The table and kitchen work well together visually. When the kitchen is shut, it looks like a simple cupboard and the table tells the style story; when it's opened up, they are a happy design duo, both playing their part in creating the complete look. Within the kitchen 'super cupboard' there are separate storage areas for foodstuffs, equipment and crockery. A full-sized fridge sits behind one of the bottom cupboard doors as well as a stack of concealed drawers, while the shelving on the inside of the bi-fold doors holds dry foods. Crockery and glasses are stashed in the deep shelves above the splashback.

This is a great example of well-thought-out kitchen design. The answer is simple...when you see it in front of you. Inhabiting only a minimal space, the kitchen becomes part of the living area, adding practical storage and workspace, and all neatly wrapped up in a high-end, well-designed structure. Moreover, it doesn't shout – on the contrary, its tone is quiet and impeccably stylish. Flooded with light, it feels comfortable – perfectly at ease with itself.

rosie wolfenden's london apartment

Many kitchens are inspired by an image in a magazine or the resident units or colour scheme when you bought your home...but this is something totally different. It isn't often that you encounter a kitchen inspired by a 1970s classic Le Creuset saucepan, but this is true of Rosie Wolfenden, the young jewellery designer and co-founder of the successful fashion jewellery company Tatty Devine. Stylish, charming and unassuming, Rosie holds this successful set of cards very lightly, even being awarded an MBE for her services to fashion.

These characteristics are evident in the design of her kitchen. When she moved into this North London apartment, the original kitchen was tatty; the oven and appliances had been removed, leaving gaping holes in the units. For a while, she coped with just a single temporary hotplate and a kettle while she agonised about what style of kitchen she wanted. She thought back to the one in her previous flat and identified two successful elements: the worktops were constructed from reclaimed school science lab bench tops, made from Iroko, a type of African teak hardwood, which is rich and dark in colour; and the beautiful ceramic wall tiles were created by a friend, the artist Rob Ryan. Those two elements, together with the classic orange cast-iron and wooden-handled Le Creuset saucepans she'd grown up with and loved, were all the inspiration she needed.

The design and layout started with a simple sketch, and the rough shape soon emerged. Rosie repositioned it away from its original dark corner to the glazed French doors overlooking the sunny, south-facing and bird-friendly garden. Together with an artisan carpenter friend, she decided that the most economical way to create the base units was to use basic carcases from Ikea and to make the doors out of plywood with an orange formica laminated surface.

style notes

There is a stylish modernity about this kitchen, and while its roots are vintage 1970s, the craftsmanly workmanship, rich deep colour and clever design essentially re-work these themes into a very contemporary space. The wall cupboards are a completely new build, made from offcuts from the teak workbench. The doors are teak framed with fluted glass centres and add lightness, texture and a period touch. The '70s-style teak cupboard handles would look at home on a mid-century teak sideboard with their sinewy, space-age influenced sculptural form. They do their job so well it's hard to tell if the cupboards are a well-made re-interpretation of an original '70s kitchen or the real thing.

The 'breakfast bar' area has a similar crafts-made approach. The stainless steel unit was part of an old catering piece, which Rosie customised by adding open-faced drawers. The plate-rack was something she'd long hankered after and she rescued it from a skip. After a scrub and re-furb, it was ready to fix to the wall. Continuing this reclaimed theme, the light fittings are upturned, fluted glass science funnels, suspended on coloured flex. They echo the glass in the wall cupboards and have their own glamour. The timeless Heals oak table was bought at an auction, and the two sturdy benches are fashioned from old floorboards.

The quarry-tiled floor came with the house, and although Rosie wasn't desperately keen at first, it's grown on her over time, as though by default. It's nice sometimes when choices are taken away from you. Her style ethic is not something seen and copied but a genuine expression of who she is. Her tastes and loves have been acquired, developed and built upon throughout her life, resulting in a comfortable home that is highly individual, quirky and inspirational.

chert modernist kitchen

At first glance, you could be forgiven for thinking this modernist building was the creation of a hip urban professional, but it was designed as the retirement home for two professional women, Miss 'Koo' Haddock M.B.E. and Miss Connie McDowell, who had enjoyed illustrious careers in engineering and science. The house took its name from the local type of flint, which was known as 'chert'. Unusual and original, it stands out from the other retirement homes on the Isle of Wight. The ladies who commissioned Chert were scientifically and technically educated and drawing on their combined wealth of knowledge, they worked with a local firm of architects, Gilbert and Hobson, between 1967 and 1970 to design and build this incredible house. Internally it is composed of two identical wings – mirror reflections of each other in layout and style. Each lady had her own upper floor bathroom, kitchen and reception rooms and shared the central 'solarium', garages and workshop where they made mosaic tiles.

The building has a cantilevered first floor, an aluminium spiral central staircase, large glass aluminium-framed sliding windows, weatherboarding and a strong horizontal theme to its design. The interior is an example of clean, simple, balanced modernism. There are no decorative architectural features; no architrave or cornices. This is an exercise in simplicity – a truly functional design built for its owners' needs. The bi-fold doors can be opened to create more communal spaces; and built-in black vinyl-topped storage units sit below the windows.

The two kitchens at the back of the building open up onto the front-facing sitting/dining rooms and benefit from the south-facing light and views. They are simple rooms, with a large fold-down cupboard that functions as a dining table or workspace. In contrast to the white and very pale grey muted décor, the beautiful aquamarine interior of the cupboard provides a welcome burst of vibrant colour.

style notes

Small space design inevitably requires some forethought in order to make the best use of the available space. Although relatively small by our modern standards, these mirror-image kitchens engage us and they open up to the living and dining areas in the building, making them great examples of a truly flexible space. Their owners planned them methodically, researching the best and most modern kitchen units of the day. These are by 'Wrighton', an English company that was much sought-after in the late '60s and '70s for its well-designed high-quality products. Like the house, they are simple; their large doors have a minimal textural finish, and there is just a single run of main units in each kitchen. Aluminium handles run the length of the top, creating a clean sleek line. The work surfaces are made of formica, with a deep squared-off edge.

The dividing wall between the kitchen and the living area contains the fridge as well as a floor-to-ceiling cupboard, whose central section has a fold-down door. By means of a simple mechanism, this door can be transformed into a dining table or a handy additional work surface. Although externally it's the same clean, crisp colour, the interior of this cupboard, together with the table and shelves, is a gorgeous and vivid aquamarine. The ladies picked up on this vibrant colour elsewhere in their kitchens. Behind the cooker in one of the kitchens is an intricate mosaic of small tiles in the same aqua mingling with white and orange tiles. Other

decorative tiles in the style of Poole pottery are set in small groups of four and interspersed amongst the plain white tiles that cover all the walls.

The flooring is uniform throughout the kitchen, dining and living areas – a very gentle and almost ethereal pale grey, flecked with black and white . The colour that you see is dependent on the way the light falls on it. Overall, the effect is of a light, breezy, fluid space, minimising any decorative separation between the different areas of this space.

The general feel of these kitchens is bright, simple and timeless, and it speaks of great quality. Despite their age, their clean lines and clever design mean these kitchens are still equally relevant in style today. Brightly coloured and referencing the period, the saucepans and storage containers provide additional bursts of colour. The place suits items, albeit period or modern, with a clean, good sculptural form; their unpretentious honesty signals modernity.

The women who commissioned this amazing mirror-image house and kitchens were true visionaries. This is a successful exercise in 1960s energy and optimism. They created a restorative space in a building that's as beautiful to look at as it is to spend time in. More than being just the perfect design for their living arrangements, it is also a bright and airy lightbox where the sea views and the seemingly infinite sky are the big players. And now you can enjoy it, too, as it was bequeathed to the National Trust and can be rented out for stylish holidays.

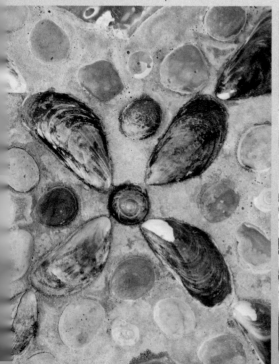

studiomama functional beauty

Designers Nina Tolstrup and Jack Mama founded their design business Studiomama in 2000. Believing that timelessness and unpretentious qualities are what are needed in design, Nina's work is simple and honest as well as playful and humorous. She created this small London rental property from a cramped inner city carpenter's workshop, which was initially so jam-packed with machinery and wood that it was almost impossible to move. Major renovation was required because the building had no proper bathroom or kitchen and the ground floor was devoid of any natural light. There was work to be done to transform this unlikely structure into the light and habitable space it is today. The ground floor was opened up with windows hidden behind wooden shutters, so that from the street outside the building looked the same and didn't lose its essential character. The back door had a glass pane added and Nina made a slot in the floor between the lower and upper storeys to share some of the upstairs daylight with the darker ground floor. She removed the entire roof, raising the walls to increase the headroom and creating sufficient space to build a mezzanine pod. Two new skylights were installed, adding a huge amount of daylight upstairs as well as enough trickle-down light to the darker ground floor.

The kitchen is sited at the back of the ground floor, with a dining table in the middle of the room and a design classic, a Hans Wegner day bed, functioning as a sofa beneath the window at the front of the building. Nina's efforts to maximise the amount of light overall transformed what had been a dark industrial-style workshop into a luminous and airy habitable space. Her philosophy is minimalist and all about staying true to the materials you're working with – the design needs to work practically and aesthetically without any compulsion to over-embellish. Consequently, there's a raw honesty in this design along with a warmth and simplicity.

style notes

This is a small space and Nina was keen to design a really simple kitchen that would blend into the main living area – just two neat runs of wall cupboards that reach the ceiling plus floor units. No frames, hinges or catches are visible, only the smooth, neat knotless planes of wood. They provide a strong-lined canvas against which the table and chairs are punctuated, and the plain splash back cuts a white horizontal plane through the warm-toned wood. It really doesn't get much simpler. The striking dining chairs didn't look like this when Nina found them in a local market. The frames were redesigned and powder-coated in a wonderful uplifting orange and the seats and backs were re-upholstered. The marble-topped kitchen/dining table with its narrow tapering legs caught Nina's eye at her children's Saturday school and she asked if she could exchange it for a new one.

Nina loves colour, but she left the walls a plain flat white, preferring to add colour in terms of art, small objects, rugs, furniture and textiles. The long orange and white geometric zig-zag rug runs most of the length of the ground floor, forming a strong graphic shape in itself, which is exaggerated by this cleanly defined pattern. The framed Jo Niemayer prints on the wall look totally at home in this space and provided Nina with not only her inspiration but also her key colours – the geometry and right-angled forms in the room are echoed in these prints.

This is an example of how design skills can play into real-life architectural and interior design. Nina's basic ethic has remained true and is visible everywhere. It's interesting to scale up your designs, retaining your principles of proportion and making things relevant, each playing its part and no more. There's nothing superfluous in this simple but truthful space.

architectural

Some kitchens go beyond style and function into the realms of architecture. They are built within the constraints and parameters of existing structures or designed to extend or complement them. I thought it would be interesting to look at what some of the masters of spatial design have created and how they use the different elements within a space, such as their exacting choice of materials and their consideration of light and movement, to see what we ordinary folk can glean from their skill and expertise.

Most of the kitchens featured here have been designed by architects, either for their personal use or for their clients. However, Antoine Vandewoude's Antwerp kitchen has been fashioned by a supreme craftsman and artist who sets the same exacting standards of design, precision and forethought. The Italian green box kitchen is a unique and imaginative glass structure, added to an architecturally unprepossessing holiday home. A surrounding framework of lightweight posts and wires clad with climbing plants and creeping foliage has created what is in effect a truly 'green' building.

The kitchen at Astley Castle blends the old with the new. The contemporary home that was built into the fabric of the ancient ruins won the 2013 Stirling Prize, one of the world's most prestigious architectural competitions. Elegant and spatially grand, this luminous open space successfully combines twenty-first century technology with traditional materials and mediaeval walls. It's an architectural gem – a bold and original scheme that's created a truly beautiful, functional and romantic space where you feel you're a part of the aesthetic.

In a converted factory apartment in central London, two talented architects transformed their industrial-style kitchen into a sleek, sophisticated space, employing an unusual mix and match approach with bespoke units and nuanced details that proclaim craftsmanship and impeccable style. Some of these builds, such as the Silver Strand Californian beach house, are jaw-dropping, but although they're the stuff of dreams for most of us there's often something appealing that we can apply and enjoy in our more modest circumstances.

silver strand beach house

This spectacular Californian beach house was designed to embrace ocean and channel views. From one elevation, it overlooks the Pacific, whereas from the diagonal there are vistas of the Channel Islands marina. Unsurprisingly, it's an award-winner with several interior design and architectural prizes. The two-storey house is smack on the sand in the surfing town of Oxnard, an hour's drive from downtown LA. Given its awesome location, the interior has been designed to reflect and engage with its exterior context. Interior designer Hailey Soren commissioned architect Robert Kerr to build a family beach getaway and the result is this imaginative home. The project was a close collaboration between them and their complementary skill sets. Hailey's strength lies in finishes and furnishings, whereas Robert's is more technical.

From the street side, there's a strong separation between the two storeys. The upper one is solid, almost heavy, where its plain grey stucco exterior takes on an asymmetrical butterfly form, echoing the shape of the lifeguard's hut down below on the beach. In contrast, the lower storey is partially wrapped in playful glass mosaic tiles with a sprinkling of gold squares that sparkle in the bright sunlight, and one corner is tiled a homogenous red. These tiles are more than just decorative – unlike painted and other delicate finishes, they can survive the weathering effects of the seafront elements of wind, water and salt. They are also an aesthetic and practical nod to the established idiom of the Californian indoor/outdoor lifestyle.

To enhance the beach house's thoughtful green credentials, the rooms have been designed so that the air flows freely throughout – there is no need here for air-conditioning or heating systems. The siting of the house and the positioning of the windows and doors all take advantage of the natural cross-ventilation of the cooling beach-front breezes.

style notes

The architecture and the location are the major players here, so just how do you tackle the design and layout of a kitchen that has to play along with these two characters? Do you compete...or take a side step...or just give up altogether and let them hold court? Between them, Hayley and Robert came up with a workable solution, which has clarity as well as a powerful aesthetic. Firstly, the interior of this building had to have a direct relationship with the exterior. The living and dining areas all face the beach, while the kitchen and breakfast nook enjoy the same unobstructed ocean panorama but from further back. In order to make this possible, the floor was raised by 35cm (14in) and the beach-front roof overhang was angled upwards to make it disappear from view when you are looking out from inside the kitchen but without affecting its function of providing shade on the wide outdoor terrace.

The daylight beautifully infuses the kitchen space through a large angular skylight in addition to the large glass doors and windows overlooking the beach. The LED linear light fittings also make a contribution. The white kitchen wall units are simple clean surfaces without details or handles – they are luminous in their stark white purity. The walnut floor cupboards and flooring ground all this lightness, and the glass mosaic tiles, which are used so effectively inside the building as well as on the exterior, harness the light and engage with it, a twinkle emanating from the gold tiles. They create a brightness that is held inside the room.

The long kitchen island serves double duty as one wall of the staircase ascending from the ground floor to the upstairs living area. The work surfaces are a clean white quartz composite

whereas, conversely to this coolness, the cabinetry is custom-made walnut. Its warm tone and grain pattern add a softness to the space and relate to the planked teak flooring.

Hayley selected some classic styles, furnishings and objects for her beach house kitchen, and then proceeded to liven them up. For the lounge area, she chose to go with the ultimate classic mid-century Californian lounge chairs. Designed in 1956 by Charles and Ray Eames, their white upholstery literally glows with light in this lightest of spaces. The round dining table is another design classic, similarly designed in 1956 but this time by Eero Saarinen, a friend of Eames, while the dining chairs are by Eames and Saarinen. The architecture, interiors and furnishings all follow suit, with cleanly defined lines and a style that is effortlessly contemporary albeit with a strong timeless reference.

Inside and out, this building's architecture and location are the stuff of dreams, but look beyond its awesome location and how it complements this, blending into the environment. Don't make the mistake of thinking that this kitchen is for someone else and not for you. Although it may seem immensely glamorous and unattainable, it also embodies simple inspiring ideas that you can translate into whatever budget space you are trying to get to work for your own needs. A good example of this approach is the simple tiling that is used in several locations throughout the house, the floors, cabinets and walls, picking a simple bright red in the chairs' upholstery and small decorative items, the exterior render and in the tiling itself. All these elementary but strong elements are used in multiple ways, helping the space to achieve its sense and look of working as a whole – and a beautiful one at that.

london architects at home

After 17 years of living in a converted 1908 factory building in the heart of central London, Christopher and James, the founders of the innovative architectural designers Project Orange, decided to give their apartment a makeover. Although the layout still worked, the kitchen, in particular, had got tired. They wanted more drama and a sense of richness without changing everything, so they asked asked a joiner they knew to build a new kitchen, choosing rosewood for the bespoke units with their medium sheen finish. Using this type of rosewood is quite unusual – and the veneer came from an old reclaimed plank – so a little has gone a long way here!

The doors open up onto the little cast-iron balcony, where you can sit outside on sunny days, but as the original metal fire escape it cannot be blocked off. Having a 'back door' in a city apartment makes a big difference. This is a sheltered spot where Christopher and James grow culinary herbs and their geraniums flower all winter long.

They strongly believe that re-working your interior should not be about slavishly following fashionable trends; rather it should be an evolution and a mood for change. Their apartment has moved from being industrial and robust in the 1990s to a sleeker, more elegant and classic space today. This kitchen exudes thoughtfulness. It's a considered space, but it's layered with a sense of time, bravely mixing different woods, furniture and objects from different periods – from the elegant antique chest, humble church chairs and working table to the high-end bespoke units. It doesn't look overworked; it's stylish and interesting.

style notes

Mixing different woods isn't easy, but here it's been spectacularly successful. The units are rosewood, the floor is oak, the antique chest of drawers is mahogany and the sliding door is oiled tulip wood. The old wooden balcony doors have been left unpainted. Dark rosewood is an unusual choice for a kitchen, but this space can take it, while the dark grey wall helps to unify everything. Painting a wall dark does not necessarily make a room dark.

The rosewood cabinets are finished with consummate craftsmanship. No awkward handles are visible – the doors have a cleverly concealed hidden pull detail at the base. It's the same with the drawers, and there are soft close hinges to prevent the doors banging. Likewise, the dishwasher and under-counter fridge are not on display and don't spoil the smooth, regular patina of the units. Even the pull-out extractor fan is neatly housed within a wall cupboard. The sink is integrated in the same Corian as the worktop and splashback, and even the tap is white. Along with the sleek cabinetry, this creates a clean uncluttered feel. The wall cabinets fit exactly into the recess area and fill it right to the top – no awkward gaps or wasted space .

Christopher and James invested in furniture that will last forever. They painted the base and legs of the stainless-steel topped table a dusty red and added church chairs. The finished look is appealing, subtle and doesn't scream, 'Look at me – I'm brand new'. The antique chest looks surprisingly cool in this contemporary setting. The lustre of the wood and absence of decorative details all resonate. This kitchen exudes thoughtfulness. It's a considered space layered with a sense of time, bravely mixing woods and furniture from different periods.

The architectural and social history of this Grade II-listed building during its eight centuries of continuous occupation is remarkable. Associated with three English queens, Astley Castle is really a 'fortified manor house' with a moat, church, lake and grounds. Unfortunately, it was gutted by fire in 1978 and was deemed to be in such a parlous state of decay that its future was beyond conventional help. A range of options was considered while the structure continued to suffer, rendering traditional restoration impossible.

Eventually, a solution emerged whereby the castle could be reinhabited while retaining the ravages of time. Thanks to a fundraising effort and lease negotiation by the Landmark Trust, in collaboration with architects Witherford, Watson and Mann, a scheme was hatched to rescue the castle. The brief was to blend the old and new, introducing into the ruins 'well-designed living accommodation that belonged unequivocally to the present day'. The imaginative house they built won the Stirling Prize 2013, a prestigious architectural competition.

The architects decided that neither a restoration nor a modern glass box was the answer. Their plan was to work within the existing ruins, blending the original walls and materials with the new, recognising that the past had a significant role to play. Some parts of the original structure could not be saved and were taken down; the exterior walls were repaired and stabilised; and a partially covered roof area was created, with the centre left open to the sky. The new accommodation was built into the older parts of the building, the brickwork 'stitched' in between ancient bricks and stones. No attempt was made to disguise it or pretend it was original...all is proudly on show to marvel at. The result feels natural and a sense of living in an 800-year-old castle, albeit with twenty-first century mod cons, still pervades this space.

award-winning astley castle

style notes

Modern, elegant and spatially grand, this kitchen puts emphasis on the choice of materials, the details of their integration and the proportions of the kitchen space within the entire upstairs living area. It's a completely open space, with views through the huge glazed panels to the Elizabethan and Jacobean ruins, which are now in effect two open courtyard and dining spaces. The living room area of the room has a large wood-burning stove, seating and vistas towards the countryside and the historic church.

It's often a challenge to furnish a really large open space – knowing where to place the pieces of furniture and establishing their correct scale, especially in such a unique setting, can be difficult. In this vast room all the diverse elements contribute to creating an incredibly comfortable and successful space. And, surprisingly, although it's grand, it's not intimidating. The muted palette of the new brickwork and old stone is continued into that of the soft furnishings, the slate work surfaces, the tiled and wooden floors, the wood of the island and the tone of the cabinetry. The large slate-topped island and eight-seating dining table create a visual balance and symmetry, anchoring each other within the space. The two modern fridges are neatly tucked away out of sight under the island, facing the cooker and counter recess.

In this kitchen, the joining and blending of old and new materials was carefully considered down to the last detail. The joints between the stones and brickwork are irregular but precise, beautiful and detailed. The old and the new are equal parties here in creating this beautiful, nostalgic and functional space. And you can enjoy the romance, too, by renting it out as a holiday home from the Landmark Trust.

woodside mid-century californian kitchen

California has a rich architectural heritage and William Wurster is one of its luminary figures. This property, which was designed by him in the 1950s, is built in his signature 'ranch style' with locally sourced materials. With its essentially simple structure, it was designed specifically to engage with the climatic conditions of the area. This example, situated in the Portola Valley just outside California's Silicon Valley, has been re-designed by the San Francisco based designer Charles DeLisle, a long-term fan of Wurster's work. Rather than set about faithfully re-creating his iconic mid-century style, he has done something radically different and new.

The house belongs to a young professional couple with children, who use it as their summer residence. DeLisle wanted to create a personal space for them with a timeless quality that could be enjoyed and appreciated by future generations and would also be sophisticated yet playful. The house is naturally light, with large glazed double doors opening onto the outside spaces. DeLisle worked with the architect Ian Moller on the project, and together they decided on the key panelling of the interior walls, using a rich, warm-toned cedar wood. This reinforces one of the major characteristics of this style of architecture: the correlation between outside and inside.

The dining chairs are a set of mid-century vintage T.H. Robsjohn-Gibbings while the table is one of DeLisle's own designs, with its modern, punchy turquoise surface (see page 102). The light fitting, hanging low over the table, is another of his unique creations with echoes of the outdoors – a geometric angular design with lights that sprout like buds on the main branch of a tree. It's supported by a hand-woven rope hanging from the ceiling.

style notes

The kitchen is part of an open-plan room – with its high wood-panelled ceiling, visible roof supports and doors into the garden, it's a light and airy space. The tiled splashback exaggerates the architectural shape and runs right up to the open wooden eaves. The colours of the tiles (terracotta, sand and gold) were part of the scheme for the house, and the earthy tones are lifted in the fabrics and hard furnishings by adding bright modern greens, pinks and turquoise.

The island unit houses the hob, and a long recess runs the length of the reverse side, under which the pink-upholstered bar stools are tucked away. DeLisle designed an asymmetric-shaped table out of a chunk of Douglas fir with proportionally thick column legs and an angled recessed edge to create a piece with a monumental quality. The white Magis chairs, with their lighter, more delicate touch and geometric cut-out backs, contrast with the visual weight of the table. The white is picked up in the layered, teardrop, organic-shaped lampshade, also designed by DeLisle. Continuing the theme of bringing the outside in, two small rectangular tables, fashioned out of raw hewn wood, are placed in front of a small pink daybed/sofa.

Set in a recess within a wall of storage cupboards is the kitchen library. Echoing the warm tones of the panelled walls and ceiling, it helps create a cohesive room, relieving the flat plane of the cupboard wall. This is a grown-up, timeless space – a kitchen designed to reflect the spectacular architecture of the building and the relationship between outdoors and indoors. The extension of the tiles and steel extractor chimney right up to the eaves makes the link visible without being pretentious. It's a slick, well-executed environment that doesn't follow trends and which reinterprets our perceptions of what constitutes a modern luxurious home.

antoine vandewoude's timeless kitchen

Sculptor, artist and furniture-maker Antoine Vandewoude creates beautiful objects of substance that evoke the passage of time. He aims for balance in everything he does and his unique Antwerp home reflects this approach, juxtaposing an interesting mix of timeless items. Many designers like their style to be instantly recognisable, but Antoine prefers his work to 'stand on its own, in such a way that you don't feel me'. After buying this slightly austere turn-of-the-century house in 2004, he gutted it and started again, making all the doors, windows and floors himself. The building had experienced various incarnations, including a stable, a taxi company and even a sweet factory. Over time, and taking his reference points from the distinctive French Quarter houses in New Orleans, Antoine created a visually rich home for him and his family via an aesthetic mixture of found and hand-crafted items.

The exterior plasterwork has been rendered in a chalky caulk, giving it the appearance of naturally aged stonework, while the paintwork is in muted, old-fashioned, matt tones. Forty-year-old Bonsai trees stand in pots on the metal balcony's balustrades. They signal the passage of time, offering a sense of stability and an asymmetric beauty. The kitchen is on the first floor at the rear, its small balcony overlooking the Japanese-inspired garden. In this light and airy open-plan room, a counter with old bakery shelves is the partition between the kitchen area and main living space. Decorated and detailed without being fussy, it feels like a well-used family kitchen. There's a large dining table and huge vintage dresser, discovered by Antoine's wife Anna in an old millinery workshop. The shelves are backed with vintage mirrors with a mottled patina to bounce more light back into the room. The work surfaces are a cool, matt, honed marble – perfect for Antoine when making his weekly batch of sourdough bread.

This kitchen is a skilled assembly of salvaged, collected, restored and craft-built pieces. It deeply references different periods of design history, weaving them seamlessly together. The floorboards are a case in point. Although it's a new floor it certainly doesn't look like it. The boards don't have parallel edges, nor are they flat – they widen or narrow slightly along their length. At first glance, they look like a regular wooden floor, but they're fitted so carefully that you don't instantly see this detail. In the past, every possible inch of wood was used, but trees are not uniformly straight like precise machine-cut planks, so the planks cut from the top of the trunk were narrower than those from further down. As Antoine says, 'Now that wood is cheaper, it's more cost-effective to make everything straight'. The floor was given an undercoat of traditional red oxide paint and a top coat of coniferous green. Over time, the top layer has worn down so the red oxide and natural grain show through.

The 1953 original metal sink units were produced by Raymond Loewy, a master of industrial design. When Antoine purchased these beauties, they were painted white and in poor condition – now restored to their former glory, they are powder-coated in a mint green. The cooker hood, designed and built by Antoine, conceals a modern unit. The mottled glass-panelled design is light and decorative and has retained the industrial and European tones of the rest of the space. Overall, the vertical height in this kitchen is used well. The huge vintage wooden glass-fronted cabinet almost reaches the ceiling, while elsewhere there are horizontal layers of textured materials, including tiles, mirrors and glass. Even the ceiling lights, three classic white glass ball fittings on chains, are hung at different heights.

green box

Having a unique place in which to follow your passions, hang out and cook, and enjoy al fresco eating is the stuff of dreams, but this incredible kitchen, which has been created within a glass box structure, with an area set aside as a gardening area/potting shed/den, really fits the bill. It's designed so the foliage can grow all over the building and it's imaginative and individual. Sited in an alpine valley, not far from Lake Como in Italy, it's a retreat for a dentist with a passion for gardening, who has been coming here since he was a child. The green box kitchen was added on to the older main house and is used mostly in the summer months.

A firm of provincial architects were briefed to create a literally 'green' building of vegetal construction. The main house has a sturdy, solid look and feel, and the idea was to continue the theme of using basic and simple materials in the design of this new glass space, while undertaking a reworking and redesign of the older property.

The main box shape of the building is divided into two sections: in the first (originally the old garage) is the kitchen area, while the second section, which protrudes, contains a little dining and gardening room with amazing views over the garden and valley beyond. Vertical rough stone pillars support the box, and the entire glass building is surrounded by a structure of custom-made lightweight galvanised posts and wires to enable the creeping foliage to grow and spread over its entirety.

style notes

The space is divided into two sections: the main area, including the kitchen, and the protruding box, which is used as a dining room area and store for gardening materials. The kitchen was designed thoughtfully using materials that are sympathetic to the exterior. The work surface is made from galvanised steel, with wide larch planks for the flooring set at a 90-degree angle to the long horizontal plane of the units and the horizontally slatted windows. The galvanised steel frame, over which the plants scramble and cling, creates the apex shape you see.

The interior is solid and uses basic materials in a minimalist style; there's steel, a locally sourced stone block wall, a textured concrete roof and glass and wood, all in cool natural tones. In an urban setting, it might seem a little harsh, but the unique expanse of visible greenery, together with the light trickling through, creates a textural warm envelope to balance the cool interior. It feels calm and part of the natural environment that surrounds you. The large sliding doors and windows are in unpainted galvanised steel, as are the custom-made taps with their simple lever controls – they have an industrial feel to them. The ceiling is concrete that has set within a wooden formwork, giving it a detailed, irregular ridged texture. The overall aesthetic was to use materials that were naturally rough and elemental.

This is an interesting project; at first glance it appears as if the encroachment of the canopy of foliage has been a happy accident of nature. Instead, the architects bravely created a unique space. Although it's been planned in a modern and imaginative style, to the un-enquiring mind there's still a remote possibility that it's been forgotten about and nature is reclaiming it.

big spaces

Most of us would love to have a large expansive kitchen, filled with daylight and with the space to cook, live and entertain in comfort. And I bet many of us have knocked down interior walls in an attempt to create such a space. Big kitchens are in fashion and everyone wants a single living, dining and cooking area where all the family can come together. The kitchen is traditionally the focal point and beating heart of every home, so it's important to get it right, stylistically, aesthetically and functionally. The architecture of some big kitchens exudes expansiveness and airiness, and the ones featured here are infinitely flexible and multi-functional. What they all have in common is an honest simplicity. Three are imaginative conversions of industrial or commercial buildings – a warehouse, cinema and British naval base – while the other is an extraordinary 'boathouse' kitchen constructed with reclaimed materials.

Marilyn retained the industrial feel of her kitchen while creating a tranquil open-plan space that is home to a collection of diverse vintage pieces. On the other side of the world in Melbourne, Hilary and Ben created a quirky yet ergonomically viable kitchen in a warehouse apartment. Despite its industrial heritage, they worked with the existing raw materials to transform an unprepossessing working environment into a comfortable and stylish space. Judy Millar's New Zealand kitchen is a masterpiece in simplicity. What makes it so special is how it fits effortlessly into the bigger picture – its remote location perched on a cliff top above the ocean. And in downtown Los Angeles, Willard Ford took on an inspiring but heart-sinkingly dilapidated 1926 cinema building. On a limited budget, he redesigned this unprepossessing space into the ultimate home/business/workspace using ideas we can apply in our more modest homes.

In every case, the kitchen feels right and it's where the owner instinctively wanted to be. In the older converted kitchens, the redesign followed an organic path rather than a 'grand plan'. These owners worked within the parameters of the existing space and its intrinsic style to accomplish their objectives. What all these spaces have in common is the ability to inspire us – to make us look and dream. Hopefully, if we get our own vast kitchens we'll have some idea of how to fill the space comfortably and make it work.

kim sing converted picture house

Located in downtown Los Angeles, this former cinema, built in 1926, is the home and gallery of Willard Ford, the furniture designer son of actor Harrison Ford. He knew the building well from his childhood, and years later he passed by and discovered it was up for sale. Ravaged by time, the once glamorous picture house was in a sorry state, dilapidated and replete with rats. However, Willard is made of stern stuff and wasn't deterred. In order to succeed, this vast space needed to be put to work and open for business, and he had to find a way to make it pay for itself. It took him four years to get planning permission to convert the building while a plan emerged for a living/working space for himself and his young son, together with a fashion, furniture and art showroom, a base for his businesses, and five street-front retail shops. The former picture house also functions as an exhibition space, which can be rented out for functions and events.

The conversion from a cinema to multi-functional mixed usage required consummate skill and imagination. A major challenge was to find an ingenious way to get enough light into a space that was designed to be dark and cavernous. Another was creating a series of level surfaces from the traditionally sloping floor of rows of cinema seating. A vast internal courtyard was created to address the issue of flooding the space with daylight, while different levels were added as a solution for the sloping floor problem. The courtyard not only functions as a light conduit but also as a natural ventilation system, which is more energy-efficient, environmentally friendly and cost-effective than installing an expensive air-conditioning system. It opens, via a series of doors and glazed panelled walls, onto the kitchen, gallery and living space.

style notes

The kitchen is an integral part of a huge space that is also used as a workspace and lounging area. Willard is a former bike racer and a collection of his bikes hangs from the wooden ceiling trusses. Don't be misled by its glamour – all this was created on a tight budget. The ideas and ambition were big, unlike the funds, and affordable solutions had to be found. The apparently 'custom-made' hi-spec and site-specific series of red lacquer posts and panels that lead off the glazed internal courtyard are, in fact, affordable off-the-peg numbers from a hardware store. They had four colours of resin-impregnated birch ply – yellow, blue, red or brown – so Willard chose red. The interior was stripped right back to the basics with its concrete floor, open ceiling vault, exposed metal ducting and raw sandblasted brickwork.

Although it's a luxury to have so much room, creating a comfortable and aesthetically pleasing living space in such a large area can be difficult. It takes courage as well as a good sense of visual balance and proportion. Don't try to work with conventional domestic-sized furniture – the result is an uncomfortable, unfocused space. Here, the opposite is true. The vast long kitchen island is in proportion to the room and balances the freestanding wall of sleek cupboards behind it, while the space between the island and courtyard doors is anchored by the dining table. The doors and glazed panels are made in a mass-produced material, but are not off-the-peg in proportion – they reach right up to the roofing joists and vertically fill the space. The distinctive red doors, red lacquer coffee table and side tables and vibrant artworks add the punch to this palette of clean, crisp rawness.

marilyn's beachfront kitchen

This extraordinary building on the seafront in Whitstable, Kent, faces out to sea. It was built in 1884 on a base of oak pillars and its concrete walls are covered with shiplapped wood cladding. It wasn't designed to be decorative – it's a purposeful place. Originally, it was used by the Royal Navy as a base for firearms training, but after this dramatic incarnation its beautiful aspect was harnessed for more peaceful purposes: as a World War I military convalescent home. It subsequently became a holiday home for disadvantaged poor inner city children.

The building is a well-known piece of local history, and when Marilyn heard it was up for sale she had absolutely no doubt – she had to have it. She sold everything she owned to raise the money to buy her favourite place in town. Garnering enough funds wasn't easy, but she bravely borrowed money from her mother and friends and eventually became the proud new owner. Every morning she got up, put on her dungarees and began scrubbing the place.

Marilyn paints in watercolour and makes items from beads and fabrics. She has always enjoyed collecting all manner of things – embroidery, ceramics, even biscuit tins or stuffed toy dogs on wheels. It is against this backdrop that she has created an amazing home. Unlike most of us, she has the courage to follow her own tastes to the limit, and everything about this place has meaning. Even the powder blue used on the walls, floor and just about everywhere isn't any old blue...Marilyn created exactly the right tone and depth of colour by mixing the paint herself.

She liked and respected the kitchen's scale and institutional catering feel. The large double doors that lead directly onto the beach have a hypnotic view, and the space opens onto a spacious dining/living area. This kitchen is the beating heart of her home – a tranquil place to sit, cook, read and create – and all set against the incredible backdrop of the sound of the sea.

style notes

In her kitchen Marilyn has a clear and decisive vision – every item within her scheme is allowed to tell its own story. The over-riding style feature is the institutional aesthetic, which permeates the structure, materials and design. The multiple catering-sized pots, pans and kettles, and collections of similar-themed pieces, such as plates, biscuit tins and vintage milk bottles, are all bound together in a glorious but restful blue. The walls, woodwork, flooring, cooker, dishwasher, heating boiler, kitchen cupboards...no architectural shape is spared. Blue – and this is a very specific shade – is the single harmonious feature that holds this diverse collection together, unifying them as a whole.

Marilyn has had the courage to go with her own taste; as an artist, the decoration of this space is paramount. Much of her inspiration came from what was already here, and its basic layout hasn't changed much. Many of the objects, such as the multitude of classic sugar pots, were in situ on the day she arrived – in its institutional days, there would have been one on each of the dining tables. Similarly, with the salt and pepper pots, Marilyn likes multiples and the story they bring with them. When she has dinner parties, every guest has their own set.

Interestingly, many objects that were in everyday use in the 1950s and '60s weren't designed with fashion in mind. Well-designed, functional and made to last, they have become design classics and their iconic shapes have become the ones we visualise for 'tea pots', 'salt pots' or 'colanders'. Marilyn appreciates the beauty and design credibility inherent in such utilitarian things. The old cooker broke down and was replaced with a new one, which sits well, with its sturdy, masculine lines and, of course, it is just the right shade of old-fashioned powder blue.

The internationally acclaimed artist Judy Millar built her unique home on top of a cliff on the rugged west coast of Auckland, New Zealand. Sitting on a 1.6-ha (4-acre) site with tracks through the subtropical gardens and bush to the black sands of Anawhata beach below, it's so remote that the nearest settlement is 30km (18 miles) away. As soon as she saw the land, Judy knew it was the perfect location for the 'boat house' she dreamt of building. Together with the architect Richard Priest, she began to plan a house that was influenced by the Werner Herzog film 'Fitzcarraldo', in which a boat was dragged through the bush. The design and building processes were highly original albeit unconventional: the plan was to source industrial and demolition materials and put them together. As Judy found and accumulated them, Richard would modify the design and work out how to incorporate them. On the upper storey they built a simple terrace with a gabled arch that echoes the design of traditional Maori buildings.

Judy likens her home to an animal that moves and makes sounds in the wind. She never feels isolated when she's there: 'I feel at the centre of things: the waves, wind and sky.' It's an energetic, wild, sometimes violent, and beautiful place. The views are spectacular and the 'boat house' blends naturally into this epic environment – it doesn't attempt to hide from it.

The kitchen, which is a masterpiece in simplicity, is basically square, but the interior wall is subtly curved in such a way that the room almost seems to embrace you. One of the side walls is composed of wooden doors, and in summer the space can be opened up and extended to become part of the exterior deck. Judy has made this stunning kitchen the heart of her home, where she not only cooks, eats and shares food with her guests but also works.

judy millar's boat house

style notes

There is little self-conciousness about this kitchen; it was designed to be a comfortable space in which to live and work, and its focus is the remote coastal location. The architecture of the space creates a feeling of airiness – there is little distraction apart from the rugged, elemental world outside. There is no overwhelming decoration and the materials are deliberately kept in their natural form, including the stainless steel catering-style work surface and open shelving, the worn enamel of the stove, and the wooden floor, table and classic Windsor chairs. The old range heats the room as well as the water in winter; in summer, Judy uses gas bottles instead as a quick and convenient source of cooking heat.

The kitchen was built around the old steel-framed windows that she discovered on a demolition site – in fact, the wall was designed to fit the windows rather than the other way round. Judy wanted a high ceiling to generate a greater sense of dimension. The light changes as each day progresses and at sunset the room is filled with amazing colours, which reflect and bounce off the walls. The tongue-and-groove floorboards, fashioned out of Kauri native New Zealand timber, came from an abandoned old wool warehouse in Auckland. Although Judy got them for nothing, she had to spend a whole month taking out the nails, one by one.

This kitchen has clean, simple lines and all the utensils are out on show, close at hand, rather than being tucked neatly away in cupboards and drawers. However, despite this, it's not cluttered and the overall feel is organic and natural. The furniture was inherited or found rather than purchased new – the kitchen table is the one Judy grew up with. Although she doesn't like the idea of sentimental furniture acquisition, she's come to love having it around.

Built 50 years ago in Melbourne, Australia, this is a hard-working, red-bricked warehouse apartment with large windows and a vaulted ceiling. Until Hilary Walker, a photographer, and her husband Ben Baldwin, a furniture designer, moved in, it had been used as a workspace and artists' studio. Their challenge was to transform this rough and ready working environment into a comfortable but stylish home. Apart from a simple glazed partition, a basic sink and a bench, there was no kitchen (or bathroom, for that matter). Although the warehouse was spartan, it had a certain charm, and Hilary and Ben were keen to play with what they had rather than rip everything out and start again. Their redesign followed an instinctive and organic path rather than a carefully thought-out grand plan.

They began by a simple process of rearranging everything until the space felt right, and it was only then that they started to consider what was missing in terms of the practicalities, such as storage, lighting and work surfaces. They added items as and when they found the right ones. Some existing pieces were adapted and reconfigured to make the kitchen more workable and ergonomic. For instance, the work surface bench, with user-friendly storage shelves beneath it, was altered to make it a more comfortable working height.

This quirky rented apartment was always going to be an industrial space. Hilary and Ben wanted to create a spacious living environment without spending large sums of money on radical changes. They felt that the bare bones of the place were good, and their goal was to create a space that was utilitarian, clean and aesthetically pleasing while accepting that it would not be pristine and perfect. They embraced eclecticism and were happy for the kitchen to be rough around the edges – as long as it was neatly arranged, too!

photographer's melbourne warehouse

style notes

The challenges of creating a stylish kitchen in a rented industrial-style building inevitably involve some careful thinking. As in any rented space, the fabric of the building can't be substantially altered or damaged, and you need to work with what you have and find a way to subtly add and make the space 'happen'. For Hilary and Ben, it was a case of figuring out how to achieve this on their budget and within the terms of the lease and leaving the property as it was. Working with the available light and the existing 'big stuff' (walls, floor and cabinet), they decided that most of the fittings in the kitchen should be in natural colours while, as much as possible, the rest of the space should be painted white to keep it neutral but bright and light. The colour would be concentrated in the details: the pots, crockery, kettle and tea towels.

It's much easier to acquire singular items when you're working within a vintage scheme; you can seek out mismatched individual objects with their own character rather than buying identical pieces or entire sets of things. This 'one off' approach of buying brightly coloured single items means that, although they are individually disparate, the overall look has a cohesive theme. In this case, it has created a bright vintage patchwork, with lots of character, against a neutral background.

The original kitchen cupboards were rather grimy, so after a good scrub and a lick of paint they were used to store cleaning materials. All the dry food plus plates, cups, glasses and cutlery are put away neatly in an antique dresser. And the cute little melamine table with 1950s-style metal hairpin legs was about to be thrown out by a friend before Hilary asked if

she could take it home instead. With a new project, or when trying to reinvent a space, most of us are familiar with the urge to rush out and buy something new straight away, but sometimes an alternative and better solution emerges if we are patient and wait a while. Hilary and Ben needed somewhere to store their pots and pans, so when a length of pipe was left over from installing a bath in the warehouse, they used it in true waste-not, want-not fashion, to create a rack, suspended from a length of natural jute rope.

However, the economies of re-using or buying items second-hand don't always run smoothly or end up saving you as much money as you envisaged – so-called bargains can be elusive. In dire need of a cooker, they found just the thing going for a song on an online auction site, but the practical and technical difficulties of fitting this vintage model ended up costing them four times as much as the amount they paid for it! Other money-saving measures, however, had less painful outcomes: even though the mismatched taps are delightfully wonky and not level, there is an unexpected joy and humour to this motley pair.

This unusual kitchen wears its heart and honesty on its sleeve. It's all about making the most of the raw materials that were already in situ, reducing waste by utilising and recycling second-hand objects and utensils, and letting your instincts and natural style lead the way. There is a confidence in leaving some things be while modifying others. Using a simple, neutral background, you can add stylish details and highly individual finishing touches to create a functional working kitchen that reflects your personality, even on a tight budget in a rented apartment.

thrifty

In times of austerity, more people adopt a back-to-basics lifestyle and embrace traditional and homely values like thrift. We are becoming more environmentally conscious and a stylish green economy is taking root, based on sustainability and fuelled by our desire to make better use of scarce resources. Practising what we preach often begins at home, and our kitchens provide the perfect space for applying these values. Instead of giving your kitchen an expensive makeover and employing professional interior designers or installing high-end units, you can work with what you've got within a budget to individualise it and create a stylish yet functional space. And you don't need a predetermined master plan – some kitchens evolve over time and are all the better for it.

The 'sharing economy', a collaborative and sustainable economic system built around sharing our assets and resources, is gaining momentum. In her seaside kitchen, Claire swaps favours with friends and craftspeople instead of paying for services and pieces – the frames of her antique mirrors were made by a metalworker in return for photographic services. Brand new is not always best. You can root around in junk shops, car boots, charity shops and skips to find beautiful pieces that can be recycled, repaired, rubbed down, painted and given a new lease of life. Sometimes it's refreshing to step outside the conventional norms and celebrate the aesthetics of mismatched crockery and vintage furniture as long as you know when to stop. In the cleverly restored Mission, original fittings and vintage units are mixed with modern ones so subtly that everything blends.

In her Copenhagen kitchen, Sabine Lavigne kept the original quirky pine units even though they weren't functional by today's standards. Finnish textile designers Saana and Olli don't spend money needlessly on new items but buy the best they can. The trend for not using new is also seen in Australia, where the owners of Tupenny Farm took furniture with cherished memories from their parents' homes and mixed them with salvaged pieces to make a farmhouse that is 'new country'. And we feature the Liverpool childhood homes of John Lennon and Paul McCartney. These are beautifully restored houses with an enormous cultural legacy. Stylistically, we see that things have gone full circle and that these ordinary kitchens from the '50s and '60s still inform our taste today.

copenhagen designer's home

Danish stylist Sabine Lavigne lives in a Copenhagen suburb in a traditional brick villa. Together with Kristine Meyer, she co-owns Meyer-Lavigne, an internationally acclaimed design partnership. When Sabine and her husband bought the house, they took down all the inner walls on the top floor to make one huge room, but this was such a big job that by the time they got round to renovating the downstairs kitchen they had used most of their budget. Forrtunately, the kitchen had enough intrinsic appeal that it didn't need too much of a spend. They gave the walls a matt whitening varnish to look lighter and replaced the cork floors with wooden ones. It's a bright and airy space and, with the doors flung open wide, it feels like you're sitting in the garden. For Sabine, it's always relaxing, whatever the weather.

style notes

Sabine's sensitivity for colour, materials and textures and the way she combines them is inspirational. This look is so low-key, natural and effortless that it doesn't appear to have been styled at all. Nothing is over-arranged and, surprisingly, she likes to integrate some clutter to create atmosphere. Comfortable and homely, the space has a reassuring simplicity and lived-in feel. The pine kitchen units with their classic brass hinges don't fit today's functional standards: the doors are too large and the cupboards too deep, but they have their own quirky charm. What's most important for Sabine are the objects that have 'been infused with time and spirit' and tell a story about the 'hands behind them'. The classic 1950s kitchen cabinet came from her grandparent's home as did the two green FDB chairs. She kept the colour because her grandmother had painted them herself.

This old wooden house in Finland is home to Saana and Olli, a young couple who design and produce their own eco-friendly textile collection. Their product values are based on timelessness and a human touch, while their design philosophy is guided by sustainability and durability. Their home adheres to the same philosophy. When they saw this house for rent, they wanted it immediately. It was the traditional kitchen/living room that won them over and they stripped it back to the basics. Spare, rustic and simple, it reflects their sustainable approach to living. To practise what they preach, they limited kitchen utensils and appliances to essentials only. Although the units weren't what they would have chosen, it was more ecologically sound to live with them than buy replacements. They tweaked them to create something more to their taste, taking the doors off some cupboards, adding black grout to the white wall tiles to create a graphic look and using black and wood as a contrast with the lighter items.

style notes

There are some charming retro touches like the picnic-style table and bench seating, the seagull lamp and the wall clock. The stove is a traditional 1940s heat-retaining model, which still works well. Scrubbed, stripped-down wood adds to the simplicity and lightness of the space. Arctic birch camping mugs with reindeer leather handles hang near the old battered stove; and the chopping boards and even the cleaning pot brushes are fashioned out of pale beechwood. The floor and waist-high wall panelling are also wooden, and a neatly stacked pile of logs stands beside the range. This room has an aura of timelessness while still managing to be stylish and elegant in its extreme simplicity.

saana ja olli
finnish eco
kitchen

island vintage 'mission'

This 'tin tabernacle' was built in 1895 on the Isle of Wight as an evangelical mission. The ministry reached out to the community, but following its heyday in the early twentieth century the membership declined and the mission building fell into disrepair. In 2007 it was put up for sale and purchased by two modern evangelists, albeit of a different persuasion but with an equal conviction – a sense of duty to the building and a vision of how it might be infused with new life. Helen and Fraser Cunningham, an ex-stylist and a photographer, had moved out of London to create and grow a business based around vintage-style holidays. The tin chapel found its saviour in this pair of visionaries who restored it as a holiday let, reflecting simpler times, and leaving intact as much as possible of the original building.

Architecturally, the couple knew that they wanted their new purchase to have that elusive 'wow' factor, even though most church conversions struggle to achieve a pleasing internal configuration that doesn't carve up the space in an uncomfortable way. It's difficult dividing such a cavernous space into useful rooms; the windows are usually very tall and don't work within a traditional two-storey structure; and there's often a bucketful of planning restrictions. Luckily, Helen and Fraser had a talented architect in the family and he suggested an ingenious solution: build a white cube within the main hall. The finished large upright 'T' structure is a clever design. In the central section, on the ground floor, is a bathroom, while upstairs, in the wider section, is a mezzanine floor with two open-plan bedrooms.

The main living space and kitchen retain a feeling of height and openness, and the integrity of the hall is preserved intact. The original kitchen was tiny and sited at the back of the church, so the decision to move it to a more spacious area, linking it to the main living space and thereby creating an easy flow between the two spaces, was a good one.

style notes

This space just feels 'right', as though it has always been here, like a church hall kitchen in which mother and toddler groups, scouts and brownies once congregated for tea and squash. But it's a new installation, which cleverly uses a mix of vintage and modern pieces. This brings its own practical and aesthetic problems: things don't always fit, colours don't necessarily match, and new items can stand out like a sore thumb. The light is quite muted inside the building, but Helen and Fraser wanted a luminous interior, so they chose a restrained colour palette and kept patterns to a minimum. Nothing heavy was imposed while well-chosen period textiles and objects provided additional visual interest. The kitchen units are classic 1950s 'English Rose', made of 'Pyluminised' aluminium on a stainless steel base. Helen sourced a couple of units locally and managed to find a job lot of matching ones. They were so well made that, apart from a couple of door catches and minimal respraying, few repairs were necessary.

The usual clutter of domesticity and decorative details is kept to a minimum. The wooden floorboards and wall panelling are original, and the horizontal planked panelling has been painted right up to picture rail height to give a unified feel to the space. The old school-style radiators are a new addition, blending in seamlessly as though they've been here for decades. The worktops on some units retain their original blue formica surface, whereas the square-edged ones are modern. Creating an authentic feel in a vintage-style kitchen is a skilled task and Helen has done this by being thoughtful and restrained. The style of the units, the original '50s curtain fabric, and the modern, retro-style fridge all tell the visual story.

RELYING ON THE LORD
CHRIST FOR SALVATION.
TRUSTING IN GOD FOR STRENG
PROMISE HIM THAT I WILL ST
TO DO WHATEVER HE WOULD
TO HIM AND READ THE BIBLE EV
DAY, AND THAT THROUGHOUT
WHOLE LIFE I WILL ENDEAVOUR
HIS GRACE, TO LEAD A CHRIST
LIFE.

AS AN ACTIVE MEMBER,

I PROMISE TO BE TRUE TO
MY DUTIES, TO BE PRESENT AT,
TO TAKE SOME PART, ASIDE F
SINGING, IN EVERY MEETING UN
HINDERED BY SOME REASON W
I CAN CONSCIENTIOUSLY GIVE T
LORD AND MASTER JESUS CHRIS
OBLIGED TO BE ABSENT FROM
MONTHLY CONGREGATION MEETI
WILL IF POSSIBLE SEND AN EX
FOR ABSENCE TO THE SOCIETY.

australian farmstead home

Located in Australia's premier Shiraz wine-producing region on Wild Duck Creek in Victoria, Tupenny Farm is a stylish smallholding. Mainly used by Paula and Antony as a weekend retreat, it is also home to a small flock of Dorpers sheep, the two alpacas that guard them, and some miniature pet goats. It was constructed back in the 1960s as a 'fibro shack' from a relatively inexpensive sheet building material that was used commonly in Australian weekend and beach shack-type properties. Originally, asbestos was utilised as the fibrous agent that bonded the cement into tough durable sheets, but this has now been replaced with a safer cellulose.

It wasn't love at first sight for the couple when they first saw this property. Their preference was to buy a plot of land and build something new, but when the additional costs of digging in mains drainage, installing perimeter fencing and bringing in utilities became clear, this simple farmhouse became ever more appealing. By the time they came back for a second viewing, its charm had grown on them and they could see the financial advantage of buying an established property and modifying it to create the weekend home they craved. The house might have been basic but at least it was in reasonable condition.

After two weekends of full-on work demolishing parts of the house that weren't to their liking, they completed the remaining major renovation and structural work within two months, including replacing the small windows with four new sets of French doors as well as the original solid doors with glazed French-style ones. However, the finishing touches took up every weekend for most of the following year. The kitchen renovation began on Day One. The couple ripped out the old one while the professionals put in the new windows and doors. Structurally, the place is four rooms: two large bedrooms, the kitchen and dining area, and the bathroom/laundry room. Large verandahs extend the length of the house on both sides.

style notes

The kitchen is charmingly simple, with rich textures and quirky details. Paula has given it a nostalgic feel to match the style of the rest of the house. It was important for her and Antony to be able to relax as soon as they arrived on Friday nights – they wanted a decorative but functional space. They could not change the position of the stove because the house is built on a large deck with a strengthened, specially constructed brick pier underneath to support its weight. They liked its vintage look, so it won its place in their remodelled home.

Paula is driven to acquire objects she responds to, hoping she can find a place for them, and the kitchen was no exception. The French doors and deep, chunky kitchen sink came from a building salvage yard nearby – luckily, they appealed to her acquisitive nature. The hefty, well-worn bench was found on Facebook, via a photographer friend who also sourced second-hand furniture, while the tall stools came from a junk shop in the nearby town of Elmore.

Painting the floor black was a brave move, but it serves as a strong base against which the shapes and textures of the rest of the kitchen stand out cleanly. The walls and ceiling were kept a simple white and the line of three identical white light fittings keeps the 'visual weight' of the room grounded by the floor and well-worn workbench. The sink counter has a row of pegged pale-striped tea towels to cover the open shelving. Crockery is kept on wall shelves. All these items have a special resonance for Paula and Antony and some are family heirlooms that were part of their childhood homes. In their new incarnation, they play their part in this modern version of a stylish retreat, creating a weekend home that provides its owners with the essential elements of rest and relaxation that are key to escaping from the stress of city life.

photographer's seaside kitchen

There comes a time in our lives when we consider moving out of the city to find more space and a restorative, gentler lifestyle. Photographer Claire Richardson's personal epiphany happened when she spotted this Regency seaside townhouse. It was love at first sight and Claire has never regretted following her heart – even though she encountered some initial problems. In her enthusiasm, she failed to spot that the exterior parapet was broken and water had been dripping down the front of the brickwork behind the render, causing the middle floor lintel to rot into dust. The upper floor joists were rotten at the front, too. Claire had let her heart rule her head and, unfortunately, she hadn't had a full structural survey of the property.

It isn't hard to see the appeal of this elegant building, built in 1835 on the East Sussex coast: the southwesterly aspect soaks up sunlight for most of the day, and the sea is visible from all three floors. However, as with many period houses, the kitchen is tucked away at the rear, overlooking a steep back garden, which is built into the cliff face. It was a dark, damp and cold room when Claire moved in – desperately in need of some TLC. Making it warm and dry was her immediate priority, and she installed a multi-burning stove. Burning wood or coal, it creates a cosy atmosphere and adds hugely to the character of the space.

Furnishing the kitchen happened organically and gradually. Claire inherited the old Habitat freestanding units, and purchased the additional steel one from Ikea. Her only other addition was the corner cupboard, which was renovated by a carpenter friend who added a new oak top. There was no master plan for creating the room – just an evolutionary process of adding things she discovered and liked. A fan of car boot sales and flea markets, she collects anything appealing. Her artworks, china and cutlery have all been acquired in this way.

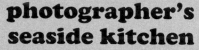

style notes

There are two major stylistic themes in this space. It has elements of a traditional kitchen with its freestanding units and collections of items, which have been acquired over time, but, unusually, it also has the feel of an art studio. The casually sited evocative vintage fruit still lifes and floral paintings contribute an unselfconcious and relaxed feel, which is quite soothing. They hang amidst and around the elements of the working kitchen – the shelves, splashbacks and cooker hood. This effectively creates an artful patchwork in which the kitchen itself plays a part.

Two strong, clean horizontal planes have been established: the cooker and the worktop surfaces; and the long horizontal shelf above the cooker. Around these, the pictures mingle with everyday functional items, such as the simple enamel jug holding wooden spoons, a small chalkboard for shopping lists and messages, an attractive old baking tin set up as an objet d'art, and a vintage radio. The art is an important element of life, not an added extra. It catches your eye, drawing you in and making you look even more closely. Observe how Claire has used reflective materials to maximum effect in the overall composition of the kitchen – a mirror-based tray set upright on the work surface, a vintage mirror-fronted medicine cabinet on the wall, and two distressed antique mirrors backed with vintage floral fabric. The metal frame was made by a local metalworker in return for some photographs. Claire says, 'I quite like to swap favours with friends instead of paying with money'. Along with the glint of the silver cutlery, these all add a lightness and energy to what was previously a dark space. To make the kitchen brighter and more luminous, she painted the walls a warm cream colour instead

of the original blue, which made it appear colder. Interestingly, she is a big fan of nearby Charleston Farmhouse (see pages 38–41), and there are echoes of its beautiful painterly style in the artful, comfortable and unpretentious atmosphere of Claire's kitchen.

She found the small classic farmhouse kitchen pitch pine table, with its turned legs and a small cutlery drawer, in a local antiques shop. Albeit small and practical for everyday use, it can be extended at either end for entertaining. It was originally bright pink in colour but its top was sanded to a natural wood finish while the legs were re-painted in a delicate 'Churlish Green' (available from Farrow & Ball). The stacking chairs, with their vintage Ercol feel, were purchased from a friend who was having a clear-out and, although Claire cheerfully admits that they aren't the most comfortable in the world, she absolutely loves them.

She likes to stack mismatched crockery, arrange diverse objects in pleasing configurations, and store cutlery upright in jugs or other containers. This, along with her accumulative tendency to buy whatever catches her eye, means that from time to time the piles get too high and an edit is needed. When this happens, she keeps her favourites and recycles the rest via her local charity shop, with William Morris's famous quote echoing in her ears: 'Have nothing in your house that you do not know to be useful or believe to be beautiful'.

This is an important lesson that we can all learn: if we want to achieve a natural and authentic feel, it's key to know when to stop so as to avoid a room looking contrived, self-conscious and over-worked. By choosing only the things that she loves but, crucially, knowing when to stand back and take an objective view, Claire can't really go wrong.

This house, on a busy road in Liverpool, was John Lennon's home from 1945 to 1963. He was five years old when he moved into Mendips, which he later described as 'a nice semi-detached place with doctors and lawyers living around'. He lived here in the care of his aunt Mimi and her husband George, who provided him with a stable, loving family life. Years later, hearing that the house was up for sale, John's widow Yoko Ono stepped in and bought the property. For her, it was the essence of his early life and, as she says, when you visit the house 'you step into John's childhood'. She wanted not only to protect it but also for the restoration to be as sympathetic and authentic as possible. It was in this house that John started to write and play his songs and it influenced his work as well as his beliefs.

Yoko bequeathed the house to the National Trust, so it could be saved for the nation and frozen in time, preserving all the details. However, there were no photographic records in existence, so family members and Mimi's student lodgers were tracked down and they contributed their recollections of what the house was like during John's formative years.

Externally, the house was pretty much as it had always been – the original windows were still intact and no major renovations had taken place. However, the interior had been neglected and there was a huge amount of work to do. The re-creation of the interior involved an exhaustive hunt for the correct period pieces. Although it was effectively a stage set, it had to live and breathe and not be a clichéd representation of 1950s life – it was essential for it to evoke the time and place and lives of its previous occupants in an authentic and credible way. The house is now Grade II-listed.

john lennon mendips

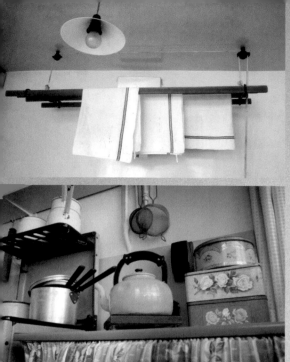

style notes

The National Trust worked with Yoko and her advisors and, little by little, the original layout of the kitchen, its style and colour palette emerged. The next step was to source the appropriate items of 1950s middle-class kitchenalia. The stainless steel sink with a double draining board was aspirational and modern in its day and, fortuitously, an electrician who worked for the Trust had an aged aunt who had just moved out of her home, leaving behind a treasure chest of domestic appliances and utensils from that period. They had been more or less untouched since the '50s and were just the right pieces to create an authentic kitchen at Mendips.

When John lived here, the back door would have been the main point of entry for the family whereas the front door was used only by important visitors, such as the doctor. This is a comfortable middle-class home with a spacious garden. The kitchen is a bright, sunny and happy family space. The small black-and-white checkerboard patterned floor and decorative curtain over the open shelves, along with the pale creamy yellow and blue paintwork and sunny yellow formica work surfaces, create a sense of optimism, stability and reassurance. The shelves form a simple dresser, where the day-to-day china was stored.

The kitchen echoes with the distinctive tick-tock of a traditional wooden wall clock, which was given to George, John's guardian. So redolent was this of his time at Mendips that he later installed the clock in the apartment he lived in with Yoko in New York. As part of the restoration, Yoko had an exact replica made and placed in its original home. As she says, 'This boy was different, but in many ways so ordinary' and the kitchen represents exactly what she means.

Paul McCartney and his family lived in this small unassuming house at 20 Forthlin Road in Liverpool between 1955 and 1964. Paul was 13 years old when they moved in, but by the time they left Beatlemania was in full swing, and the huge numbers of fans drawn to his home were making life difficult for the McCartneys. This was a time in post-war Britain when rationing was coming to an end, unemployment was relatively low and a house-rebuilding project was underway. Prosperity was starting to return. Paul's mother Mary was a health visitor and midwife on a modest income and couldn't afford to buy a home, but wanting to do her best for her family she got the tenancy of this terraced three-bedroom council house.

It was a time of domestic innovation, too, and the kitchen in this typical working class house benefited from the new labour-saving equipment that was becoming widely available. Once the exclusive preserve of the wealthy, these domestic appliances were now aspirational objects for many ordinary households, and Paul's family were no exception. The twin tub washing machine, cooker and fridge were essential components of a modern lifestyle.

The McCartneys were a creative family: Paul's dad played the piano and he encouraged his sons to play instruments. Mike, Paul's younger brother, was a photographer. His documentary-style images of family life are displayed on the walls of the sitting room and helped inform the restoration. This house, where the writing partnership between Paul and John Lennon began, was acquired by the National Trust due to its significant place in the history of twentieth-century popular culture. The restoration was aided by a grant from the National Lottery. The kitchen is a small room at the back of the house, overlooking the garden, and the backgrounds of Mike's photographs provided accurate information for the restorers. The house is Grade II-listed and open to specially arranged tours.

paul mccartney
20 forthlin road

style notes

This is a simple, practical kitchen, and from our contemporary perspective of relative luxury and our modern re-interpretation of 'retro', it is startling in its simple charm. We still admire the simple yet austere style of kitchenware, such as the white enamel cookware with a blue line edge, butler's sink, brown betty teapot, formica-topped table and linen tea towels. We love them for their integrity, their genuine aesthetic, and the sense of kinship they bring.

Laundry would have been hung on the wooden airer, then hoisted up to the ceiling by a pulley and sash cord to dry out of the way. In those days, any individual creative impulses were limited to choosing the fabric for the curtains, the trim on the edge of the shelves and the 'home maker' crockery of the time. In those days, council houses came painted in a limited range of colours decided by the local authority – here, it's 'council house cream'.

None of this would have been uncommon in kitchens of that era. It was a period of great social and economic progress, and these are the beginnings of the modern kitchen as we know it. But given its provenance as the kitchen where John and Paul would have brewed up a cup of tea and made a sandwich, it's incredibly evocative. It's important to preserve it for the sense of the passage of time that it gives us, as a window into the enormous social changes that the middle part of the twentieth century brought, and as a fascinating glimpse into our social history. From this humble start, but with the strong interaction of family bonds, friendship, music and photography, life took an incredible path, and it's great to look back at the small details of where it all began and realise that although times are very different now, our tastes haven't really changed much at all.

sourcebook

antiques

Robert Gordon
www.robertgordonhome.com
email: rob.gord@blueyonder.co.uk
tel: 07771995118
Warehouse: 60 Rochester Place
London NW1 9JX

architects

act romegialli
(Green Box)
www.actromegialli.it

Nicolas Hugon with Stephane Maupin and Partners
(Mathieu Mercier)
www.stephanmaupin.com

Robert Kerr
(Silver Strand) Based in Santa Monica, California. A multi-disciplinary architecture and design firm
www.rkad.com

Richard Priest
(Judy Millar) Architecture that leans towards the contemporary, but allows the site and client brief to direct the development of any project
www.richardpriest.co.nz

Project Orange
(Eaton Terrace & Bannen St) Award-winning RIBA Chartered Architect and Interior Design Studio
www.projectorange.com

Witherford Watson Mann Architects
(Astley Castle)
www.wwmarchitects.co.uk

designers

Lucie Allison
Children's accessories designer
www.lucieathome.com
Email: l-allison@live.co.uk

Katrin Arens
Furniture and clothes designer
www.katrinarens.it

Hive Haus
Bespoke modular living spaces
www.hivehaus.co.uk

Charles de Lisle
Original jewellery design lighting and objects for the home
www.charlesdelisle.com

Virginie Manivet
Home stylist & personal shopper
www.virginiemanivet.com

Meyer-Lavigne
Quirky ceramics, porcelain, textiles, glass, wood and print
www.meyerlavigne.dk Net shop:
www.meyerlavigne.bigcartel.com

Saana ja Olli
Sustainably produced interior textiles from Finland
www.saanajaolli.com

Socia Design
Boutique interior design studio in San Francisco
nicole@sociadesign.com

Studiomama
Product range includes materials recycling and extending product life.
www.studiomama.com

Tatty Devine
Original jewellery design
www.tattydevine.com

interior designers

Abigail Ahern
Interior design and shop
www.abigailahern.com

Hannotte Interiors
Toronto-based design firm with a collective of skilled trades, artists, crafts people and sources
www.hannotteinteriors.com

Kaisa Luukkanen
Designer and Interior Architect based in Helsinki, Finland
www.kaisaluukkanen.com

retailers and suppliers

Crea Diffusion
Corian worktops and sinks
www.crea-diffusion.com

Ducksoup Maui
Balinese furniture, art and home accessories
2000 Mokulele Hwy, Puunene, Hawaii 96784
www.ducksoupmaui.com

DuPont
Corian worktops and sinks
www.dupont.com

ferm LIVING
Danish-designed interiors,
home products and wallpaper
www.fermliving.com

In This Street
Art, fashion and objects
12 Smith Street, Collingwood, Victoria,
Australia
www.inthisstreet.com

Sokeva-käsityö
Hand-made products by visually
impaired craftspeople in Finland
www.sokevakasityo.fi

kitchens to visit

Astley Castle
A Landmark Trust property. Available
to book for holidays. There are footpath
trails around the wider site of the
castle, which are open all day every day
www.landmarktrust.org.uk/our-landmarks/
properties/astley-castle-683

Boulevard Leopold
Bed & Breakfast accommodation in elegant
nineteenth-century Antwerp House
www.boulevard-leopold.be

Castles in the Sand
Holiday villas to rent in Essaouira,
Morocco, through Emma Watson
www.castlesinthesand.com

Charleston
A Bloomsbury house and garden
www.charleston.org.uk

Chert
A National Trust property.
Available to book for holidays
www.nationaltrustcottages.co.uk

Forthlin Road
Paul McCartney's childhood home in Liverpool.
A National Trust property
www.nationaltrust.org.uk/beatles

Kim Sing Theatre
A dynamic event space in Los Angeles for
exhbitions, brand events and private parties
www.kimsingtheatre.com

Mendips
John Lennon's childhood home in Liverpool.
A National Trust property
www.nationaltrust.org.uk/beatles

The Modern House
Studiomama designed house to let
in Bethnal Green, London E2
http://www.themodernhouse.net/holiday-lets/
bethnal-green/description-813/

Tupenny Farm
Rent an Australian fibro shack on
a farm at McPhersons Lane,
Mia Mia, Victoria 3444, Australia
www.airbnb.com.au/rooms/893965

Vintage Vacations Ltd
Stay in The Mission and other unusual
accommodation, including Airstream
caravans, on the Isle of Wight
www.vintagevacations.co.uk

photographers

Hilary Walker
Photographer based in Melbourne, Australia
www.hilarywalker.com.au

Claire Richardson
Photographer based in Sussex, England
Australiawww.clairerichardson.com

artists

David Bromley
Innovative Australian painter
www.davidbromley.com.au

Ann Field
Award-winning collages and illustrations.
Based in Santa Monica, California
www.annfield.com

Mathieu Mercier
Paris-based internationally acclaimed artist
www.mathieumercier.com

Judy Millar
Based in Auckland, New Zealand and Berlin.
Works on paintings and installations
judymillar.com

Marilynn Phipps
marilyn@thebattery.info

Yuge Yu
Fashion designer
www. yugeyu.com

credits

We would like to thank all the owners for allowing us
to feature and photograph their cool kitchens:

Abigail Ahern www.abigailahern.com
act romegialli architects: gianmatteo romegialli,
    angelamaria romegialli, erika gaggia www.actromegialli.it
Lucie Allison lucieathome.com email: l-allison@live.co.uk
Katrin Arens www.katrinarens.it email: info@katrinarens.it
The Battery: Marilyn Phipps, marilyn@thebattery.info
Boulevard Leopold B&B www.boulevard-leopold.be
David & Yuge Bromley www.davidbromley.com.au,
    www.inthisstreet.com, www.yugeyu.com
Charleston www.charleston.org.uk
Chert www.nationaltrustcottages.co.uk
David Easton & Cynthia Wright www.rammedearthworks.com
www.watershedmaterials.com
Ann Field www.annfield.com
Robert Gordon www.robertgordonhome.com
    email: rob.gord@blueyonder.co.uk tel: 07771 995118
    warehouse address: 60 Rochester Place London NW1 9JX
Olaf Hajek www.olafhajek.com
Jenn Hannotte Principal of Hannotte Interiors www.hannotteinteriors.com
Barry Jackson www.hivehaus.co.uk
Robert Kerr Architecture Design www.rkad.com
Paula Kilpatrick and Antony Elliot Tuppenny Farm
    https://www.airbnb.com.au/rooms/893965
The Landmark Trust www.landmarktrust.org.uk
Sabine Lavigne & Michael Strange plus Mingus and Sofia
    Meyer-Lavigne www.meyerlavigne.dk
Net shop: www.meyerlavigne.bigcartel.co
Charles de Lisle www.charlesdelisle.com
Kaisa Luukkanen www.kaisaluukkanen.com
Virginie Manivet www.virginiemanivet.com
Mathieu Mercier www.mathieumercier.com
    & Moraima Gaetmank www.studio-kinetique.com
Mendips & Forthlin Road The National Trust
    www.nationaltrust.org.uk/beatles
Judy Millar Artist www.judymillar.com
The Mission Vintage Vacations Ltd, www.vintagevacations.co.uk
Gunilla (physiotherapist and Feldenkrais practitioner)
    & Sven Montan MD, PhD
Nicole Socia email: nicole@sociadesign.com
Project Orange www.projectorange.com tel: 020 7739 3035
Claire Richardson www.clairerichardson.com
Saana ja Olli www.saanajaolli.com
Nina Tolstrup & Jack Mama www.studiomama.com
Antoine Vandewoude www.antoinevandewoude.com
Hilary Walker www.hilarywalker.com.au
Emma Wilson www.castlesinthesand.com
Rosie Wolfenden www.tattydevine.com

All photography by Richard Maxted unless otherwise stated.
www.maxted.com

Front cover	Ben Anders Photography
Endpapers	Photography: Richard Maxted www.maxted.com
	Studio facilities: Seamus Ryan www.seamusryan.net
	Retouching: Hank Gidney hank@mnkyldn.com
Page 1	Johan Rosenmunthe http://www.rosenmunthe.com
Pages 6,9,10	Art Gray, Art Gray Photography, 171 Pier Ave #272, Santa Monica, CA 90405, amatgray@aol.com www.artgrayphotography.com
Pages 12–15	Art Gray, Art Gray Photography, www.artgrayphotography.com
Pages 16–17	Christian Schaulin/Kerstin Rose medienservice
Pages 18–21	Jack Hobhouse www.jackhobouse.com
Pages 22–23	Angus Fergusson Inc., www.angusfergusson.com
Pages 24–25	Office photos: Aukusti Heinonen: aukusti.heinonen@gmail.com Woodworkshop photos: Riku Pihlanto: riku.pihlanto@gmail.com
Pages 26–27	Photography: Magdalena Björnsdotter Styling: Helena Blom
Pages 28–29	Jordi Canosa www.jordicanosa.com
Pages 30–31	Luke White Photography www.lukewhite.com
	Birgitta Drejer www.sistersagency.com
	Stylist: Nathalie Vei
Pages 42–43	Toby Scott www.tobyscott.com.au
Pages 52–55	Art Gray, Art Gray Photography, www.artgrayphotography.com
Pages 82–85	Ben Anders Photography (& page 4)
Pages 88–91	Art Gray, Art Gray Photography, www.artgrayphotography.com
Pages 92–95	Jack Hobhouse www.jackhobouse.com
Pages 100–103	Art Gray, Art Gray Photography, www.artgrayphotography.com
Pages 108–111	Marcello Mariana, www.marcellomariana.it (& page 86)
Pages 114–117	Art Gray, Art Gray Photography, www.artgrayphotography.com
Pages 122–125	Mary Gaudin www.marygaudin.com (& page 110)
Pages 126–129	Hilary Walker www.hilarywalker.com.au
Pages 132–133	Johan Rosenmunthe http://www.rosenmunthe.com
Pages 134–135	Mirva Kakko/SKOY
Pages 136–139	Holly Jolliffe www.hollyjolliffe.co.uk
Pages 140–143	Eve Wilson www.evewilson.com.au
	Styling: Lucy Feagins www.thedesignfiles.net
	Additional photography: Paula Kilpatrick
Pages 144–147	Claire Richardson www.clairerichardson.com (& page 130)
Pages 148–155	©National Trust Images/Arnhel de Serra/ Dennis Gilbert
Page 160	Art Gray, Art Gray Photography, www.artgrayphotography.com

acknowledgements

Like the other books in this series, this has been a great project to work on, and I'm very grateful. Not only do they allow me creative self-expression but they also give me the chance to work with my wonderful team, from Fiona Holman at Pavilion to Heather, Emily, Rachael and Sarah. I'm grateful to you all. Richard Maxted, too, my long-term photographer friend, whose sharp eye and generous nature have been called upon more than once in my career. He was not only a fantastic travelling companion but took some great images. I think he enjoyed it, too – I caught him more than once kissing the camera. And a special thank you to our US photographer Art Gray – his work is immaculate and it's an honour to have included his images in this book.

And, of course, these books are always a journey in more ways than just the physical one. The trail involved meeting and spending time with some amazing kitchen owners, who were far more than politely hospitable and accommodating. It was an enriching experience to talk to them and share their inspirations and domestic achievements. They each came with a great tale, which I hope you enjoy, too, via the words and images in these pages. Thank you all.

Jane Field-Lewis

Jane Field-Lewis is a stylist for film, photography and TV and is also the creative consultant behind the hit C4 series *Amazing Spaces*. Her work is truly global – both her styling work and books are internationally successful. She has written and art directed *my cool caravan*, *my cool campervan* and *my cool shed*, and co-authored with the architect and television presenter George Clarke the books to accompany the *Amazing Spaces* TV series.

She has an enduring love for people and style, believing that the two are closely entwined. Her career is based on the aesthetic, whether high- or low-style, and across people and objects. With her styling work, *Amazing Spaces* and *my cool...* she hopes to inspire an affordable, individual and creative approach to any project.

Additional captions: page 1 copenhagen designer's home; pages 2–3 chert modernist kitchen; page 4 marilyn's beachfront kitchen; page 6 Art Gray/LA Palms; page 9 Art Gray/LA Palms; pages 10–11 Art Gray/LA Palms; pages 32–33 charleston bloomsbury style; pages 56–57 rosie wolfenden's london apartment; pages 86–87 green box; pages 112–113 judy millar's boat house; pages 130–131 photographer's seaside kitchen; page 160 ann's los angeles kitchen

First published in the United Kingdom in 2014 by
Pavilion Books Company Limited
1 Gower Street
London WC1E 6HD

Copyright © Pavilion Books 2014
Text copyright © Jane Field-Lewis 2014

Editorial Director Fiona Holman
Photography by Richard Maxted and Art Gray
Styling by Jane Field-Lewis
Design Steve Russell
Editor Heather Thomas

ISBN 978-1-909-10879-0

A CIP catalogue record for this book is available from the British Library.

10 9 8 7 6 5 4 3 2 1

Reproduction by Dot Gradations Ltd, UK
Printed and bound by 1010 Printing International Ltd in China

This book can be ordered direct from the publisher at www.pavilionbooks.com